Essentials of Legal Services

Edward Stone
MA (Oxon), Solicitor (non-practising)

CILEX | Education

Disclaimer

ISBN: 978-1-911713-98-2
E-ISBN: 978-1-911713-99-9

First paperback edition 2025

Layout by codemantra U.S. LLC

The publisher has no responsibility for the continued existence or accuracy of URLs for external or third-party internet websites referred to in this book, and does not guarantee that any content on such websites is, or will remain, accurate or appropriate.

British Library Cataloguing in Publications Data
A catalogue record for this book is available from the British Library

Published by CILEX Education in the United Kingdom.
CILEX Education
2nd Floor,
The Pinnacle,
Midsummer Boulevard,
Milton Keynes,
MK9 1BP

Cover image: Wera52/iStock

www.cilex.org.uk

Printed and bound by CPI Group (UK) Ltd, Croydon, CR04YY

This book contains FSC certified paper and other controlled sources to ensure responsible forest management.

FSC www.fsc.org MIX Paper from responsible sources FSC® C013604

About the Author

Edward Stone is a qualified solicitor who has worked as a private client solicitor in Cirencester, preparing wills and administering estates. He has also lectured at Gloucestershire College of Arts and Technology on a variety of CILEX courses.

Since 1997, he has been working as Editorial Manager at CILEX Law School. He has written and edited a number of CILEX Law School course books covering English Legal System, Public Law and Wills and Probate. He also wrote the University of London Public Law subject guide in 2015. He is now working as a Publisher at CILEX.

Guide to the Book

Aims of chapter!

We define the learning objectives at the start of of each chapter so you understand what you are expected to learn before engaging with the content.

Key cases!

We have highlighted important cases that relate to the learning throughout the textbook.

Reflective question!

This book contains reflective questions, positioned at key points throughout the text. These allow you to take time to reflect on what you have learnt, ensure that you have understood the concepts, and contextualise your learning.

Terminology!

These terminology boxes will introduce commonly used legal terms that you may not have come across before.

Practice link!

Here we use real life explanations or scenarios which give you the opportunity to contextualise what you have learnt and explore legal concepts in a real-world setting.

Activity!

Here you are presented with activities which engage you with the content and help you to develop research skills, explore topics in more depth and consolidate your knowledge.

Law in context!

Fictional scenarios run through some chapters, helping to provide context to the material.

Useful link!

We have linked to useful websites that provide further information and helpful resources to further your studies.

Summary!

The key points of the chapter are summarised at the end to reinforce your understanding before moving on to the next topic. The summaries can also be used for quick revision.

Knowledge checks!

At the end of each chapter you will be tested on your knowledge of what you have just read. Knowledge check answers can be found at the back of the book.

Contents

Table of Cases

Section

Table of Statutes

Conventions

Table of Secondary Legislation

CHAPTER 1

The Nature and Structure of Law

Aims of chapter!

This chapter will enable you to:

- Outline the nature of law in England and Wales
- Outline the nature of primary and secondary legislation
- Outline the role of case law
- Outline the significance of international law in England and Wales

- Outline the significance of the European Convention on Human Rights
- Explain how law is classified, and
- Explain the nature of a legal person.

1.1 Introduction

This chapter aims to introduce you to the basic framework of English law. We will look first at what law is, before going on to examine the key sources of law in England and Wales. We will then go on to look at some of the ways in which we classify the law, and some of the key distinctions which may be drawn within the study of law and legal systems, which will underpin your studies as they progress.

As you develop your understanding, you will see that the legal system of England and Wales is an evolving and developing creature. It reflects the history and even geography of the United Kingdom as well as the messiness of its politics. Remember, sometimes there will **not** be a logical reason for some of its features. As your understanding of the material in this textbook develops, you may find yourself watching the news and seeing it in a new light.

A note on jurisdiction

The United Kingdom contains three separate legal systems. England and Wales are one **jurisdiction** (an area within which a particular legal system applies) although the impact of devolution is introducing specific changes to Welsh law which may, in time, lead to a more distinct Welsh legal system. Scotland is a separate jurisdiction, and Northern Ireland is a third.

Confusingly, all three legal systems (England and Wales; Scotland; and Northern Ireland) share a single **Supreme Court**, the Supreme Court of the United Kingdom, which hears cases from all three jurisdictions. This textbook deals primarily with the legal system of England and Wales, but it is important to be aware that Scotland and Northern Ireland have their own legal systems with distinct rules, processes and courts.

1.2 What is law?

The question "what is law" is both simple and complex. In one sense it looks as though the answer is straightforward: law is a system of rules which regulate behaviour. Law is all around us and governs all sorts of aspects of our daily lives, from driving a car to buying a pair of shoes. Yet when we examine the question more carefully, it becomes more complex. Not all rules that regulate behaviour are law: schools also have rules, as do football clubs and social media platforms. The rules of all these organisations regulate our behaviour, and we (usually!) modify our behaviour to ensure we abide by these rules, because if we do not, we might be expelled from school, not allowed to play football, or have our social media accounts suspended. Yet none of these rules are law.

One of the key defining characteristics of law is that it is created and enforced through governmental institutions. Laws are created by institutions of the state. These institutions include the courts, the police and a number of other organisations such as local councils.

In order to understand more about what law is, therefore, we need to look at where law comes from. In the following sections we will examine the key sources of law in England and Wales.

1.3 Legislation

One of the most important things to learn as a student of law is where the law comes from. Where do we find out what the law is? The most important source of law in England and Wales is **legislation**.

Legislation is what most people would think of if you asked them for an example of law: a written set of rules, made by a body that has authority to do so (a legislature). There are two main types of legislation in the UK: **primary legislation** and **secondary legislation**.

1.3.1 Primary legislation: Acts of Parliament

Primary legislation is the term used to describe the main laws which are passed by the legislative bodies in the UK. Within the UK, and England and Wales, most primary legislation is contained in **statutes** or **Acts of Parliament**. An Act of Parliament is the highest (most authoritative) form of law in the UK. The making of Acts of Parliament is a key function of the UK Parliament.

Acts of Parliament set out the framework and broad principles for a law. For example, the **Public Health (Control of Disease) Act 1984** sets out a framework for action that can be taken in response to outbreaks of infectious diseases and provides powers to ministers to take various actions, including making **secondary legislation** (rules and regulations).

1.3.2 Secondary legislation

Secondary legislation is legislation which provides the detail of how the Acts of Parliament will operate. It is sometimes called **delegated legislation**.

Secondary legislation is not made by Parliament, but by government ministers or other bodies (such as Transport for London), though

Parliament does scrutinise secondary legislation. Secondary legislation comes in different forms, though rules and regulations are probably the most common types, but broadly speaking it supplements primary legislation, providing practical measures that allow the law to be enforced, come into effect or be amended.

1.4 Case law

The second key source of laws within England and Wales is **case law**. Case law is law which is created by judges. Judges set out the reasoning underpinning their decisions in individual cases in **judgments** and these judgments, taken together, create a body of case law. Judgments are then relied upon by judges deciding later cases with similar facts. The decision (or judgment) in each case forms part of the law.

In theory, the role of the judge in a case is to **apply** the law, rather than to make new law. In most cases the existing law is clear, and it is easy to apply statutes and existing case law to the facts of a new case. However, sometimes the legal principles may not be clear, or there may be some aspect of the facts that is novel and has not been addressed by the existing law.

Key cases!

Airedale NHS Trust v Bland [1993]

Tony Bland was the 96th victim of the Hillsborough Stadium tragedy when he was crushed and suffered catastrophic and irreversible damage to the higher functions of his brain. This "persistent vegetative state" left him unable to move, see, hear or communicate in any way. He was kept alive by food and liquid supplied through a tube into his nose and stomach. After three and a half years in this state the hospital, with the support of the patient's family, applied to the court for a declaration (a form of court order) permitting it to cease providing food and liquid artificially and to allow him to die.

The House of Lords did not have clear law to follow in this case (see https:// www.bailii.org/uk/cases/UKHL/1993/17.html), partly because medical developments had only fairly recently enabled doctors to keep alive patients who would, in the past, have died shortly after their injuries. At the same time, there was no prospect of any improvement in Tony Bland's condition and his family and doctors believed it was not appropriate to keep him alive in this state.

The House of Lords considered several legal and ethical issues in this case. First, it looked at the principle of the sanctity of life, noting **Art 2 European Convention on Human Rights** (the right to life) but highlighted that this right could be limited by the principle of self-determination or autonomy. Tony Bland was, of course, unable to state his own wishes so the court also considered what were his "best interests", taking into account his quality of life.

Ultimately, the court held that withdrawing food and liquid was permitted in this case and Tony Bland was allowed to die.

NB Everyone now has the right to make an "advance decision" stating their wishes in relation to life-sustaining treatment – see https://www.nhs.uk/conditions/end-of-life-care/advance-decision-to-refuse-treatment/ - an option which was not available to Tony Bland before his injuries.

1.5 International law

Legislation and cases are **domestic** sources of law: they are concerned only with the jurisdiction in which we reside, England and Wales; other jurisdictions have their own legislation and may rely on cases to a greater or lesser extent. However, we should also be aware of another form of law and the influence it has in England and Wales.

International law consists of the rules and principles governing relations between states, between states and individuals, and between international organisations. As such, international law regulates not only the jurisdiction of England and Wales, but many jurisdictions around the globe. It is important to be aware that the term "international law" does not indicate a single unified system, but many different systems governing different areas.

1.5.1 The European Convention on Human Rights

One of the most important international legal systems of which the United Kingdom is a part is the **European Convention on Human Rights (ECHR)**. The **ECHR** is an international treaty which protects fundamental human rights. It has its own court, the European Court of Human Rights. The **ECHR** is a cornerstone of human rights protection within the UK and has been incorporated into UK law through the **Human Rights Act 1998**.

Reflective question!

Download the Teaching Resources "The European Conventionon Human Rights - Rights and freedoms in practice" (2013) at https://edoc.coe.int/en/educational-tools/5327-teaching-resources-the-european-convention-on-human-rights-rights-and-freedoms-in-practice.html .

Read the page headed "What is the ECHR?". Can you explain what a "Convention" is?

1.5.2 The European Union

From 1973 to 31 December 2019, the UK was a member of first the European Economic Community, and later the European Union. The European Union has its own legal system, which is a unique form of international law in that it is automatically binding in the domestic legal systems of the EU's member states. While the UK was a member of the EU, UK citizens could seek remedies in UK courts on the basis that EU legal obligations had been breached (this was known as the doctrine of **direct effect**). Now that the UK is no longer a member of the EU, the legal principles that bound the UK by EU law no longer apply, though the **European Union (Withdrawal) Act 2018** incorporated (included) all EU legislation that was in force at the time of exit into UK law.

1.6 Classifying the law

Law can be classified or grouped in different ways. We use classifications and groupings to help us understand the law better. Be aware that some of the terminology used to classify law has several meanings, depending on what it is being contrasted against.

1.6.1 Public law and private law

All law can be regarded as either **public** or **private**. Public law is that part of the law which is concerned with the relationship between the state and private persons. Human rights law is a form of public law: it defines the rights which individuals can assert against the state.

Private law is that part of the law which is concerned with the relationship between private persons. The law of contract is part of private law: it provides a framework for people to regulate their agreements with one another and resolve disputes.

1.6.2 Criminal and civil law

One of the most important ways we classify law is into **criminal law** and **civil law**. **Criminal law** is "the body of laws owed to society as a whole". It is that part of the law which enables the state to deter and punish crime. **Civil law** is the "body of laws dealing with the rights and duties owed by individuals and organisations to each other". It covers a wide range of areas of law, including property law, family law and the law of contract. Understanding whether a case is a matter of criminal law or civil law is important, because the criminal and civil court systems are separate. Cases are heard in different courts and follow different procedures. The personnel involved in the case are different, as are the outcomes.

Terminology!

"Civil law" has several different meanings depending on the context. Watch out for alternative meanings later in this textbook.

(1) Criminal cases

Here, legal action is initiated by the state. Most criminal cases are **prosecuted** (brought to trial and argued in court) by the **Crown Prosecution Service** (CPS). The **burden of proof** in a criminal case is on the prosecution, that is, it is for the prosecution to prove their case and the guilt of the defendant. The standard of proof (the "weight" of evidence which is required for one party to win the case) in a criminal trial is **beyond reasonable doubt**, that is, the magistrates or jury must be sure of guilt before convicting. If found guilty, the **defendant** in a criminal trial will be sentenced with a fine, community service or prison.

Full code test

In most cases, the Crown Prosecution Service decides whether or not to prosecute a case on the basis of the Full Code Test which is set out in the Code for Crown Prosecutors. The test consists of two stages: the evidential stage and the public interest stage.

First, a prosecutor must be satisfied that enough evidence exists to provide a realistic prospect of conviction against the suspect. A realistic prospect of conviction is defined in the Code for Crown Prosecutors as:

> *"an objective, impartial and reasonable jury, bench of magistrates or a judge hearing a case alone, properly directed and acting in accordance with the law, is more likely than not to convict the defendant of the charge alleged".*

That assessment is to be based on an objective assessment of the evidence, including the impact of any information put forward by the suspect. The prosecutor should consider whether the evidence presented is admissible, credible, and reliable.

If a case does not pass the evidential threshold, it must not be prosecuted regardless of how serious or sensitive the allegation is. If the evidential stage is met, the prosecutor will go on to consider the public interest test. Both tests must be passed for the suspect to be charged and the case prosecuted by the CPS.

If there are public interest factors/concerns that suggest that the benefits of prosecution would be outweighed by other factors, the case should not proceed. Factors that will be considered during the public interest stage are:

- the seriousness of the offence;
- the suspect's level of culpability;
- the harm caused;

- the suspects' age/maturity at the time of the alleged offence;
- the impact of the offence on the community;
- the proportionality of prosecution; and
- whether sources of information require protection.

Reflective question!

Public interest test – assisted dying prosecutions

Review the following guidance to CPS prosecutors on the application of the public interest test in relation to the offence of encouraging or assisting suicide (see paragraphs 36-48) - https://www.cps.gov.uk/legal-guidance/suicide-policy-prosecutors-respect-cases-encouraging-or-assisting-suicide .

Do you think this guidance is appropriate? Are there any factors you would include or exclude?

(2) Civil cases

Here, legal action is initiated by the **claimant**, that is, the person who believes they have been wronged. The burden of proof lies with the claimant, but the standard of proof in civil trials is different from criminal ones. In a civil law case, the standard of proof is **on the balance of probabilities**, which requires the court to find one party's evidence more convincing than their opponent's. This is a lower threshold than beyond reasonable doubt. If a claimant in a civil law case wins, the defendant is liable to provide a remedy: this is often (but not always) in the form of **damages**.

Terminology!

In older cases students will find references to **plaintiffs** instead of claimants.

1.7 Legal persons

An important idea to understand before embarking on further study of law is that of **legal persons**. A legal person is a person or organisation which is able to act in law. We use the term "legal persons" because not all those capable of acting in law are human beings. Companies, partnerships and many government agencies are legal persons: they can enter into contracts, buy and sell property and take legal action in court, just as a **natural person** (i.e. a human being!) can do.

The concept of legal persons (or legal personality) is useful, because it enables companies and other organisations to act independently of the people who run it. This means, for example, that if a company acts in breach of contract, it is the company which is sued rather than the individual directors or shareholders, and any damages must be paid from the company's assets or by the company's insurance: the shareholders who own the company and the directors who run it will not be personally liable for the company's wrongdoing. Many of the legal cases you will encounter during your studies will feature legal persons.

Knowledge checks!

(1) Which of the following statements about criminal law and civil law are correct?

(a) Criminal cases are usually prosecuted by the Crown Prosecution Service

(b) The standard of proof in a civil case is beyond reasonable doubt

 (c) The normal remedy in a civil law case is a fine
 (d) The burden of proof in a criminal case is on the prosecution

(2) Which of the following are primary legislation?
 (a) Civil Procedure Rules
 (b) Law of Property Act 1925
 (c) Categories of Casino Regulations 2008
 (d) Value Added Tax Act 1994

1.8 Summary!

(1) A jurisdiction is an area within which law applies. The United Kingdom contains three jurisdictions: England and Wales; Scotland; and Northern Ireland. Our focus in this guide is on English and Welsh law.

(2) Defining what law is, is complicated, but broadly speaking, law is a system of rules which aim to regulate behaviour, which are created and imposed by the state.

(3) A key source of law is **legislation**. Acts of Parliament (or statutes) are primary legislation: they set the overarching principles of a law. Secondary or delegated legislation supplies the detail.

(4) Case law is made by judges when they give judgment in a particular case. This creates new rules which apply in future cases with similar facts.

(5) The most important aspect of international law for the United Kingdom is the **European Convention on Human Rights** which has been brought into UK law by the **Human Rights Act 1998**.

(6) Important distinctions can be drawn between public law and private law, and between criminal and civil law.

(7) Companies and other organisations may have **legal personality**, which means they may undertake (and have imposed upon them) legal obligations.

CHAPTER 2

The Personnel of the English Legal System

2.1 Introduction
2.2 The legal professions
2.3 Summary!

Aims of chapter!

This chapter will enable you to:

- Describe the role of chartered legal executives, including qualification and areas of work
- Describe the role of solicitors, including qualification and areas of work
- Describe the role of barristers, including qualification and areas of work

2.1 Introduction

The purpose of this chapter is to look at the people who work within the legal system. We start with the branches of legal profession: those who carry out legal work on behalf of clients, including representing them in court. We will look at the areas of work carried out by chartered legal executives, solicitors and barristers.

2.2 The legal professions

The legal profession in England and Wales is divided into three main branches:

- chartered legal executives;
- solicitors; and
- barristers.

It is not uncommon for lawyers to be divided into separate categories in other countries, but it is important to realise that the divisions in England and Wales largely reflect historical developments. Although each branch has its own system of regulation and representative body, there are increasing overlaps in the types of legal work which their members carry out.

2.2.1 Chartered legal executives

There are approximately 17,000 chartered legal executives who work mainly in law firms, as well as in local government and a wide variety of other organisations. They have to complete a rigorous qualification route and develop high levels of professional expertise in their chosen specialist areas of practice. They are represented by the Chartered

Institute of Legal Executives (CILEX) (www.cilex.org.uk) and regulated by CILEX Regulation.

2.2.1.1 Qualification

One of the distinguishing features of the qualification route for chartered legal executives is the number of different entry points which are available. Students are able to complete all their legal studies through the CILEX route or to fill in the remaining gaps after studying for a law degree or other qualifications. This flexibility has been hugely valuable to many mature students who often have family and work commitments which make traditional law degrees less attractive.

The qualification framework for chartered legal executives is the CILEX Professional Qualification (CPQ). There are three stages of qualification: CPQ Foundation, CPQ Advanced and CPQ Professional. Qualification is competency based, and at each stage trainees are required to evidence both theoretical understanding of the law and practical application of their knowledge in a professional setting.

The CPQ is structured to enable trainees to specialise by completing modules in the following Pathway practice areas:

- Dispute Resolution and Litigation;
- Criminal Litigation;
- Residential Conveyancing;
- Commercial Conveyancing;
- Employment Law;
- Business and Commercial Law;
- Family Litigation;
- Wills, Probate and Private Client;
- Immigration Law.

One of the key features of the CPQ qualification is the emphasis placed on ethics and professional responsibility. Trainees are required to complete modules covering the regulatory structure of the legal profession and the CILEX Code of Conduct, as well as other compliance responsibilities in areas such as money laundering and client due diligence. Case studies are used to enable students to apply these ethical and regulatory principles to practical situations.

Further details of the CPQ qualification are available at https://www.cilex.org.uk/cilex_lawyer/about_cpq .

2.2.1.2 The work of chartered legal executives

The majority of chartered legal executives work in law firms as partners or employees, working with solicitors, paralegals and support staff. They work directly with clients as **fee earners** using their professional skills to advise a wide variety of clients, including individuals, companies and other organisations. Other chartered legal executives work in legal departments of companies, local councils, central government and other organisations.

More senior chartered legal executives have management responsibilities, including supervising junior staff and developing their firm's marketing strategy through social media.

Terminology!

Fee earner: in most law firms there is a key distinction made between fee-earners and **non-fee earners**. Fee earners (the lawyers, including trainees) will be required to record the time they spend on individual cases and the clients' bills will reflect the hourly rates for which their time will be charged. Non-fee earners, who include secretaries and accounts and other support staff, are not usually required to record their time.

The main types of work carried out by chartered legal executives (including trainee legal executives) are:

- conveyancing – buying and selling houses and flats and commercial property (e.g. shops and offices);
- litigation – this includes completing court procedures and forms as well as rep- resenting clients in court hearings;
- wills and probate – drafting wills and winding up the financial affairs of people who have died;
- family – divorces and disputes involving children and finances when relation- ships break up, including representing clients in court hearings; and
- employment – disputes between employers and employees, including representing clients in court and tribunal hearings.

In addition, some chartered legal executives work in other areas such as criminal litigation and company law.

Chartered legal executives working in organisations which are regulated by CILEX Regulation are required to comply with the **CILEX Accounts Rules** which highlight the importance of keeping clients' money separate (in a "client account") from the firm's own money – see https://cilexregulation.org.uk/entity/rules/ . Similar rules apply to all staff working in law firms which are regulated by the Solicitors Regulation Authority.

2.2.1.3 Rights of audience

(1) **Civil litigation**

All chartered legal executives who have completed the Civil Litigation Pathway in the CPQ qualification are entitled to represent clients in chambers (uncontested hearings) in the County Court and High Court. On completing an additional civil proceedings advocacy skills course, they can represent clients in the following courts and tribunals:

- open County Court hearings;
- Magistrates' Court - all civil and enforcement cases;
- Tribunal hearings; and
- the Coroner's Court.

(2) **Criminal litigation**

On completing an additional criminal proceedings advocacy skills course, chartered legal executives who have completed the Criminal Litigation Pathway in the CPQ qualification are able to represent clients in the following courts:

- Magistrates' Courts;
- Youth Courts;
- Crown Court or High Court - chambers hearings for bail applications;
- appeals to the Crown Court or committals for sentencing in the Crown Court;
- Coroners' Courts.

(3) **Family litigation**

On completing an additional family proceedings advocacy skills course, chartered legal executives who have completed the Family Litigation Pathway in the CPQ qualification are able to represent clients in the Family Court.

2.2.2 Solicitors

Solicitors are the largest branch of the profession with approximately 143,000 members in England and Wales. They work with clients in a wide range of areas of law, including conveyancing (buying and selling houses) and litigation. Solicitors are regulated by the Solicitors Regulation Authority.

2.2.2.1 Qualifying as a solicitor

Students are now able to qualify by completing the Solicitors Qualifying Examination (SQE). The requirements are as follows.

(1) **Degree (or equivalent qualification or work experience)**

The degree may be in any subject.

(2) **SQE1 assessment (functioning legal knowledge and practical legal skills assessment)**

The SQE1 assessment is centrally set and administered on behalf of the SRA, rather than by individual universities or other course providers. There will be several opportunities to sit it each year. It will consist of an assessment of "functioning legal knowledge" (FLK) with the following features:

- FLK1: Business Law and Practice; Dispute Resolution; Contract; Tort; Legal System of England and Wales; Constitutional and Administrative Law and EU Law and Legal Services.
- FLK2: Property Practice; Wills and the Administration of Estates; Solicitors Accounts; Land Law; Trusts; Criminal Law and Practice.
- 2 x 5-hour assessments over two "non-consecutive" days.
- 180 single best answer questions per assessment/day.

Students must pass both FLK1 and FLK2 to pass SQE1. Further details are available at https://sqe.sra.org.uk/exam-arrangements/assessment-information/sqe1-assessment-specification .

(3) **SQE2 assessment (practical legal skills assessment)**

SQE2 may only be attempted after SQE1 has been passed. Students will be given a written and oral assessment of legal skills covering:

- Client interview and attendance note/legal analysis; advocacy; case and matter analysis; legal research; legal writing; legal drafting.

The following practice areas will be assessed:

- Criminal Litigation (including advising clients at the police station);
- Dispute Resolution;
- Property Practice;
- Wills and Intestacy, Probate Administration and Practice;
- Business Organisations, rules and procedures (including money laundering and financial services).

Written exams are taken over three half-days. Oral assessments are taken over two half-days. For further information see https://sqe.sra.org.uk/exam-arrangements/assessment-information/sqe2-assessment-specification .

(4) **Qualifying work experience**

Students must have at least two years' qualifying work experience. As well as including the traditional **period of recognised training** as a trainee with a law firm, a wider range of experience, including as a paralegal, will be accepted.

(5) **Admission as a solicitor**

On completion of the training contract, the trainee will be **admitted as a solicitor**. The trainee's name will be added to the **solicitors' roll** (a register of all qualified solicitors).

Further details of the SQE are available athttps://www.sra.org.uk/become-solicitor/sqe/ .

2.2.2.2 The work of solicitors

The majority of solicitors work in partnerships (also known as **firms**). The partners in the firm own the business and their personal incomes depend on the profits generated by the business. The firms will employ professional lawyers, including chartered legal executives, assistant solicitors, paralegals and support staff.

Solicitors are also able, subject to certain conditions, to practise in limited companies and limited liability partnerships (LLPs). These types of organisations provide greater financial protection for the solicitors owning the business in the event of commercial failure.

Solicitors are able to work with non-lawyers in organisations called **alternative business structures** (ABSs) to provide legal services. ABSs include **multi-disciplinary practices** (MDPs) in which legal services are provided with other professional services, such as accountancy. There are a number of commercial advantages for ABSs over traditional partnerships: it can be easier to raise outside capital to fund an expansion of the business, and clients may welcome "one-stop shops" where they can get a number of different legal and non-legal services from the same organisation.

Some solicitors work as **sole practitioners** running their own business and taking all the financial risks (and profits) themselves. In rural areas, many firms operate with a number of branches in different locations. These firms will often specialise in areas such as conveyancing, wills and probate and family law. Firms working in the inner-city areas may specialise in criminal work, although cuts to legal aid have made this work increasingly unprofitable.

Many large firms use the internet and call centre arrangements to seek clients from across the country, especially in areas such as personal injury litigation and conveyancing. Other large firms, based in the City of London, carry out commercial work for very large companies, including multinationals.

2.2.2.3 Rights of audience

All solicitors are able to represent their clients in Magistrates' Courts, the County Court, the Family Court, the Intellectual Property Enterprise Court, tribunals (a more informal type of court) and Coroner's Courts (which determine the cause of a person's death).

Solicitors who specialise in litigation may choose to obtain the **Higher Rights of Audience Qualification** and become **solicitor advocates**.

Solicitor advocates are able to represent clients in the Crown Court, High Court, Court of Appeal and Supreme Court.

2.2.3 Barristers

Barristers are independent legal advisers whose main focus has traditionally been on **advocacy** (representing clients) in the courts. They are the smallest branch of the profession (approximately 16,000).

2.2.3.1 Qualifying as a barrister

There are five stages of training to be a barrister:

- the academic stage;
- admission to an Inn of Court;
- the vocational stage;
- the call to the Bar; and
- pupillage.

(1) **Academic stage of training**

All students must complete either a qualifying law degree or a degree in another subject followed by the Graduate Diploma in Law/Common Professional Examination. The degree classification must be **at least a 2(ii)**.

Some students undertake an optional one- or two-week **mini-pupillage** during this stage which gives them useful work experience with a barrister.

(2) **Join an Inn of Court**

There are four Inns of Court: Middle Temple, Inner Temple, Gray's Inn and Lincoln's Inn. Inns of Court are non-academic societies which provide educational activities and support for barristers and student barristers. They all provide the use of a library, lunching and dining facilities, common rooms and gardens.

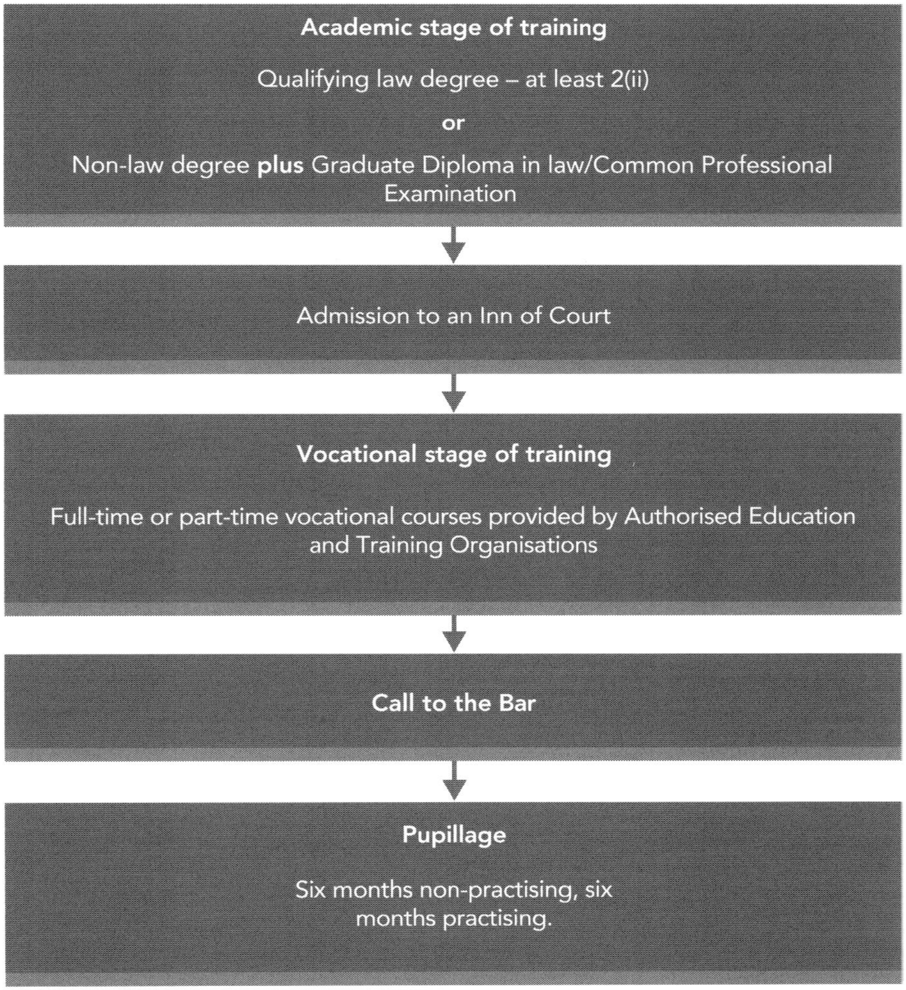

Figure 2.2.3.1

(3) **Vocational stage**

Students must apply for a vocational course at one of the universities and institutions accredited by the Bar Standards Board (Authorised Education and Training Organisations). These courses may be full-time or part-time. The courses include training in important skills, including advocacy, written skills and legal research.

At the same time, students are required to complete 12 qualifying sessions at their Inn of Court. These consist of a variety of educational and social activities, including dinners with legal talks and other events also attended by qualified barristers.

(4) **Call to the Bar**

Students who have passed the vocational stage will attend a ceremony at their Inn of Court in which they will be formally **called to the Bar**. At this point they will be entitled to call themselves a barrister.

(5) **Pupillage**

In order to be able to practise, every barrister must then complete a year of **pupillage** (practical training) under the supervision of an experienced barrister known as a **pupil supervisor**. The first six months are non-practising – the pupil "shadows" their pupil supervisor. During the second six months, the pupil may, with the permission of their pupil supervisor, provide legal services and appear in court.

Further information about qualifying as a barrister is available at https://www.barstandardsboard.org.uk/training-qualification.html .

2.2.3.2 The work of barristers

The majority of barristers are self-employed but share offices, known as **chambers**, in London and other major cities. Office expenses and support services are shared, as are the costs of the **barristers' clerk** who is responsible for allocating work and negotiating fees on behalf of the barristers. Their work consists of advocacy – speaking in court in a wig and gown on behalf of their client. In addition, they will carry out legal research on complex points of law and prepare written **opinions**, applying their research to the circumstances of their clients. Sometimes barristers will advise the clients in person – **in conference**. Barristers will usually specialise in one or more areas of law.

Barristers working in chambers have traditionally received work in the form of **instructions** from law firms. Individuals and organisations are now also able to instruct barristers directly (not via a law firm) under a **public access** scheme.

Barristers are also employed by the Crown Prosecution Service, local government and industry and commerce. They are able to work with other lawyers and non- legal professionals in organisations established under the known as **legal disciplinary practices** and **alternative business structures**.

Experienced barristers are able to apply for appointment as **King's Counsel** (KC). They are also referred to as "silks" because they wear silk gowns. (Barristers who are not KCs may be referred to in court as "juniors" – even though they may be very experienced.)

2.2.3.3 Rights of audience

Barristers have full rights of audience in all the courts of England and Wales.

Knowledge check!

(1) Which is the largest branch of the legal profession?

(a) Solicitors

(b) Barristers

(c) Chartered legal executives

2.3 Summary!

(1) There are three distinct branches of the legal profession in England and Wales: chartered legal executives, solicitors and barristers. Each has distinct but overlapping roles and distinct qualification systems.

(2) Chartered legal executives work in a variety of organisations, including law firms, local councils and central government. Some chartered legal executives become partners in firms and take management responsibilities.

(3) Chartered Legal Executives qualify through the CILEX Professional Qualification (CPQ), which is a flexible, competency-based framework. Its features include specialist pathways in different practice areas. Chartered legal executives are then able to undertake additional advocacy training in civil litigation, criminal litigation or family litigation leading to advocacy rights in the lower courts.

(4) Most solicitors work in partnerships (law firms), but some work within other organisations. Solicitors have rights of audience in some of the lower courts, in particular, the County Court and Magistrates' Courts. They are able to obtain the Higher Rights of Audience Qualification and become solicitor advocates. This entitles them to represent clients in all courts.

(5) All solicitors are required to gain a degree (or equivalent), then take the Solicitors Qualifying Exam and undertake a period of supervised work.

(6) Barristers are self-employed but work together in shared offices (chambers). They are supported by a barristers' clerk who negotiates fees on their behalf with law firms. Some barristers receive instructions directly from clients under a public access scheme. The main elements of a barrister's work are advocacy and preparing written opinions on legal cases.

(7) A prospective barrister must gain a degree in law (or an equivalent post-graduate qualification) before taking the Bar Professional Training Course and completing a period of work under supervision, known as pupillage.

CHAPTER 3

Regulation and legal services

Aims of chapter!

This chapter will enable you to:

- Describe how chartered legal executives, solicitors and barristers are regulated
- Explain the role of the Legal Services Board
- Describe the role of the Office for Legal Complaints and the Legal Ombudsman, and
- Explain the professional ethics requirements which lawyers must comply with.

3.1 Introduction

This chapter is concerned with the regulation of the legal professions and legal services in England and Wales. It starts with an explanation of the regulators for the different branches of the legal profession. We then look at some of the overarching regulators and the rules which all legal professionals, and sometimes non-legal professionals, have to abide by. We will then look in detail at some of the regulations themselves, considering the professional duties they impose in specific areas.

3.2 Regulation of legal professionals

3.2.1 Chartered legal executives

Chartered legal executives are regulated by **CILEX Regulation**. All members of CILEX are required to comply with the **CILEX Code of Conduct** which requires that they must, at all times, ensure public confidence in themselves and their profession and avoid disreputable conduct.

The **Code** is based upon nine principles, which state that members of CILEX must:

- uphold the rule of law and the impartial administration of justice;
- maintain high standards of professional and personal conduct and justify public trust in you, your profession and the provision of legal services;
- behave with honesty and integrity;
- comply with your legal and regulatory obligations and deal with your regulators and ombudsmen openly, promptly and co-operatively;
- act competently in the best interests of your client and respect client confidentiality;

- treat everyone fairly and without prejudice;
- ensure your independence is not compromised;
- act effectively and in accordance with proper governance and sound financial and risk management principles; and
- protect client money and assets.

The **CILEX Code of Conduct** (see https://www.cilex.org.uk/about_cilex/the_code_of_conduct/code-of-conduct) explains the principles by way of outcomes which members of CILEX must comply with. For example, in relation to the first principle, the outcomes are:

> "You must:
>
> 1.1 Understand and comply with your primary and overriding duty to the court, obey court orders and do nothing which would place you in contempt.
>
> 1.2 Not knowingly or recklessly allow the court to be misled."

CILEX Regulation's Disciplinary Tribunal has wide ranging powers to punish members of CILEX and firms regulated by CILEX Regulation including fines of up to £100,000 for CILEX members.

Chartered legal executives who work in law firms regulated by the Solicitors Regulation Authority are also governed by the **SRA Standards and Regulations**.

Practice link!

Chartered legal executives' continuing professional development (CPD)

During each CPD year (1 October to 30 September) members and fellows of CILEX are required to complete an online logbook recording a number of **entries** detailing planned and unplanned

activities. Planned activities include attending courses and training webinars. Unplanned activities should reflect learning experience on the job and must show evidence of some self-evaluation by the member or fellow.

Further details are available on the CILEX Regulation website.

3.2.1.1 Regulation of legal practices

CILEX Regulation regulates some legal practices run by chartered legal executive litigators and advocates, conveyancing practitioners, probate practitioners and immigration practitioners as well as those run by other "authorised persons" (including solicitors).

Legal practices (also referred to as "entities") are required by CILEX Regulation to appoint the following key personnel (one person may have more than one role):

- an approved manager;
- a compliance manager; and
- an accounts manager.

These managers are required to demonstrate competence in practice management and accounts management.

3.2.2 Regulation of solicitors

Solicitors and their employees are regulated by the **Solicitors Regulation Authority (SRA)**. Its functions include:

- setting the standards for qualifying as a solicitor;
- drafting rules of professional conduct;

- providing ethical guidance;
- administering the solicitors' roll;
- investigating complaints against solicitors and prosecuting them in the Solicitors' Disciplinary Tribunal; and
- where necessary, closing down law firms to protect the public.

The **SRA Standards and Regulations** include the following **principles**.

You act:

- in a way that upholds the constitutional principle of the rule of law, and the proper administration of justice;
- in a way that upholds public trust and confidence in the solicitors' profession and in the legal services provided by authorised persons;
- with independence;
- with honesty;
- with integrity;
- in a way that encourages equality, diversity and inclusion; and
- in the best interest of each client.

The **SRA Standards and Regulations** include the **SRA Code of Conduct for Solicitors** and the **SRA Code of Conduct for Firms**.

The SRA can impose disciplinary sanctions, including financial penalties of up to **£25,000**, on individual solicitors, their employees and firms. The SRA can impose financial penalties on **alternative business structures** (ABS) (see **2.2.2.2**) of up to £250 m and financial penalties up to £50 m on staff working in an ABS.

Activity!

Go to the **Code of Conduct for Solicitors** at https://www.sra.org.uk/solicitors/standards-regulations/code-conduct-solicitors/ .

Find **para 3.2** in **Section 3**: Service and competence. What standard of service to clients is required?

3.2.2.1 Solicitors' continuing professional development (CPD)

The SRA website sets out a "statement of solicitor competence" which defines the "continuing competences" which all solicitors are expected to meet. They include "Maintain the level of competence and legal knowledge needed to practise effectively, taking into account changes in their role and/or practice context and developments in the law…". Linked to the statement of solicitor competence is a "threshold standard" which sets out the levels of competence and legal knowledge to be expected of a newly-qualified solicitor – see https://www.sra.org.uk/solicitors/resources/continuing-competence/cpd/competence-statement/ .

The SRA website gives guidance on maintaining a "development record" of learning and development activities. Taking these documents into account, solicitors are required to make an annual CPD declaration that they have considered their learning and development needs for that CPD year and have taken appropriate measures for maintaining their competence.

3.2.3 Regulation of barristers

Barristers are regulated by the **Bar Standards Board** (BSB) which publishes a **Code of Conduct** for barristers.

The Code of Conduct covers rights of audience, advertising and relationships with solicitors. The **Core Duties** set out in the Code require barristers not to discriminate unlawfully against anyone. In addition, the Code states that barristers should *provide a competent standard of work to each client.*

In addition, barristers should not act in a way which brings the profession into disrepute. They should act with honesty and integrity and are bound by a duty of confidentiality to the client. Crucially, a barrister must observe their duty to the court in the administration of justice.

3.3 Other bodies which regulate the legal provisions and legal services

3.3.1 The Legal Services Board

The Legal Services Board has the overall responsibility of overseeing legal activities in England and Wales. It is independent of government and works with the approved regulators of the different branches of the legal profession to meet the following regulatory objectives set out in **s1(1) Legal Services Act 2007**.

- Protecting and promoting the public interest.
- Supporting the constitutional principle of the rule of law.
- Improving access to justice.
- Protecting and promoting the interests of consumers.
- Promoting competition in the provision of services provided by lawyers.
- Encouraging an independent, strong, diverse and effective legal profession.

- Increasing public understanding of the citizen's legal rights and duties.
- Promoting and maintaining adherence to (following of) professional principles.

3.3.2 The Office for Legal Complaints

The Office for Legal Complaints supervises the Legal Ombudsman – a body which is required to resolve complaints about legal services free of charge for individuals, small businesses, charities, clubs and trusts.

The Legal Ombudsman is staffed by a chief ombudsman and three ombudsmen. Complainants must try to resolve their complaints with the legal professional concerned before using the Legal Ombudsman.

It aims to resolve complaints quickly and informally and can require both parties to co-operate. It can award up to **£50,000** in compensation.

Reflective question!

Go to the Legal Ombudsman website at https://www.legalombudsman.org.uk/information-centre/learning-resources/signposting-consumers-to-the-legal-ombudsman/ .

Read the guidance to legal professionals on "signposting" the Legal Ombudsman to clients. When should clients be signposted to the Legal Ombudsman?

3.3.3 Financial Conduct Authority (FCA)

The Financial Conduct authority (FCA) is the regulator for the provision of financial services in the UK. The FCA regulates the activity, rather than a particular profession. A list of regulated activities is set out in the **Financial Services and Markets Act 2000** and includes services such as advising on investments and providing credit references.

Some of the work undertaken by the legal profession is also considered a regulated activity by the FCA. For example, if you were acting for a client in the purchase of a house, and there was some defect in the title (a potential source of liability for the purchaser), you might arrange indemnity insurance on your client's behalf. The purchase of the indemnity insurance is a regulated financial activity.

In order to undertake regulated financial activity, a provider of legal services either needs to be registered with the FCA under the **Financial Services Act 2021** or be covered by an exemption. There is an exemption under the **SRA Financial Services (Scope) Rules**, which permits those regulated by the SRA to provide financial services which are incidental to the provision of legal services. The exemption does not operate if the financial service is unconnected to the provision of legal services: for example, a law firm would not be covered by the exemption if they started offering loans or dealing in shares. It is important that you understand whether your own firm meets the requirements under these rules.

Reflective question!

Go to the Financial Conduct authority Financial Services register at https://www.fca.org.uk/firms/financial-services-register .

If you intend to deal with a new financial adviser, what should you be checking for as you use the register?

3.4 Regulatory safeguards and professional ethics

3.4.1 Personal responsibility for compliance with regulatory requirements

Lawyers regulated by the **CILEX Code of Conduct** or the **SRA Code of Conduct for Solicitors** have personal responsibility for ensuring they comply with regulatory requirements.

3.4.2 Compliance with the principles of the SRA Code of Conduct for Solicitors

The **SRA Standards and Regulations** contain the main rules and regulations affecting solicitors and other lawyers working in firms regulated by the Solicitors Regulation authority. In particular, it contains seven mandatory (compulsory) principles, the **SRA Code of Conduct for Solicitors**, the **SRA Code of Conduct for Firms** and the **SRA Accounts Rules**. An online version which reflects the latest changes is available at https://www.sra.org.uk/solicitors/standards-regulations/ .

There are seven mandatory principles which apply in relation to **all** the elements of the **SRA Standards and Regulations**. These are the key ethical and professional requirements for all firms and individuals who are providing legal services. If two or more principles come into conflict, the principle taking precedence is the one which best serves the wider public interest in the circumstances.

These mandatory principles apply in relation to **all** the elements of the **SRA Standards and Regulations** and must therefore be considered in relation to all ethical issues. The principles are set out at **3.2.2** above.

The **SRA Code of Conduct for Solicitors** and the **SRA Code of Conduct for Firms** are extensive and should be read independently. The two Codes of Conduct are aimed at different audiences, but overlap a great deal. The SRA website provides links to further commentary and guidance. In this course book, we will focus on the requirements of the **SRA Code of Conduct for Solicitors**.

3.4.2.1 Who is the client?

The **SRA Code of Conduct for Solicitors** refers constantly to the duties owed by solicitors to their clients. **Para 8.1** requires that *you identify who you are acting for in relation to any matter*. It is very important to be clear from the beginning of a case precisely who is your client. Consider the following example:

Law in context!

Darius and his wife, Ariadne, have recently attended an interview with you and have asked you to prepare wills for them both. Their instructions are clear and, although Ariadne has clearly taken charge, you have no reason to doubt that Darius is happy with the provisions of his will. Two days after you have sent the draft wills to Darius and Ariadne to approve, you get a phone call from Ariadne. She asks you to alter a legacy of £500 to her friend, Persephone, increasing it to £1,000. "And Darius wants me to tell you he wants to give his car to his friend, Xerxes."

What should you do?

The key point to remember is that, although Ariadne **is** your client, she is only your client in respect of her **own** will. You need to get Darius to confirm that he **does** want to give the car to Xerxes.

Note **Principle 3** requires that you act "with independence".

3.4.2.2 Maintaining trust and acting fairly

paras 1.1–1.4 SRA Code of Conduct for Solicitors set out the obligations of solicitors and their staff to maintain the trust of their clients and act fairly towards them, including not discriminating by allowing personal views to affect professional relationships (**para 1.1**), not abusing your position by taking unfair advantage of clients (**para 1.2**) and not misleading your clients, the court or others (**para 1.4**).

3.4.2.3 Competence

paras 3.1–3.6 SRA Code of Conduct for Solicitors concern the competence of solicitors and their staff to undertake the work they have been instructed to do. This includes an obligation to ensure you are competent to undertake the work instructed and maintain your own professional knowledge and skills (**para 3.3**) and to ensure those you supervise are competent to undertake the work instructed and maintain their knowledge and skills (**para 3.6**).

3.4.2.4 Conflicts of interest

paras 6.1–6.2 SRA Code of Conduct for Solicitors deal with the obligations of solicitors and their staff to avoid conflicts of interest between the solicitor and the client and also between clients.

(1) **Conflicts between solicitors (or their staff) and clients**

Para 6.1 applies: *You do not act if there is an own interest conflict or a significant risk of an own interest conflict.*

(2) **Conflicts between clients**

Para 6.2 states:

You do not act in relation to a matter or particular aspect of it if you have a conflict of interest or a significant risk of such a conflict in relation to that matter or aspect of it, unless:

(a) the clients have a substantially common interest in relation to the matter or the aspect of it, as appropriate; or

(b) the clients are competing for the same objective, and the conditions below are met, namely that:

(i) all the clients have given informed consent, given or evidenced in writing, to you acting;

(ii) where appropriate, you put in place effective safeguards to protect your clients' confidential information; and

(iii) you are satisfied it is reasonable for you to act for all the clients.

The most common example of where the requirements of **para 6.2** are met is the normal practice of lawyers acting for clients purchasing a house **as well as** acting on behalf of the bank or building society lending them the purchase price (the mortgage). Both the purchasers and the bank/building society have a **substantially common interest** in ensuring that the legal title to the house is satisfactory.

(3) **Handling conflicts of interest in practice**

Consider the following situations.

(1) Catriona is asked to prepare a will by Miriam, an 80-year-old client who has become very fond of her. Miriam wants to leave her entire £500,000 estate to Catriona.

(2) Rina is acting for Carlo and Fernando who have been accused of assault. They initially both plead not guilty, but Carlo later decides to change his plea to guilty and blames Fernando for starting the assault.

(3) Anna is asked by her client, Joachim, who is buying a £250,000 house from Sven, if she can do the conveyancing for both of them to save money.

What should Catriona, Rina and Anna do and how should they explain their decisions to the clients?

(1) Catriona must refuse to prepare Miriam's will. She should thank Miriam for her kindness and explain that if Miriam really wants to make a will in her favour, she must go to another law firm who can give her independent advice (see **Principle 3**).

(2) Rina cannot continue to act for Carlo and Fernando as their interests are now clearly in conflict. In fact, she will almost certainly have to refuse to act for either of them because it will be very difficult to avoid breaching her duty of confidentiality by referring to information which the other client disclosed. She needs to explain to Carlo and Fernando that she simply has too much information from each of them to be able to continue to represent only one of them fairly.

(3) Anna must explain to Joachim that she is simply not permitted to act for both parties in these circumstances. She should explain that this enables her to ensure that **his** interests are her highest priority. It is clear that Joachim and Sven will not have a "substantially common interest" (**para 6.2 SRA Code of Conduct for Solicitors**).

3.4.2.5 Confidentiality and disclosure

Solicitors and other lawyers regulated by the SRA owe their clients a **duty of utmost confidentiality**. This means that they must keep confidential all the details of their clients and ensure that their staff do likewise. Consider the following examples of where this duty is breached.

(1) Anya tells a persistent local reporter the phone number of her client who has just been acquitted of murder.

(2) James accidentally pulls out a conveyancing file of Peter Greene from his filing cabinet before he finds Paula Green's will file. He leaves Peter's file on his desk with the label visible during Paula's interview.

(3) Megan is asked to administer Sean Poole's estate by his widow and executor, Fiona Poole. She is phoned by Sean's son, Patrick, who asks who the executor is under Sean's will. She initially refuses to tell him but when Patrick says he will know soon enough when the will becomes public knowledge at probate, she tells him. She later finds out that Patrick and his parents have not talked to each other for 10 years because of a family dispute over a piano.

What should Anya, James and Megan have done?

(1) Anya should simply have refused to disclose the phone number. Reporters have thick skins and are used to rejection!

(2) James should have taken more time before Paula's interview to tidy his room and put away Peter Greene's file.

(3) Megan should have refused to say who Sean's executor was. Her reply should have been carefully worded so as not even to disclose whether the executor was male or female. She could have offered to ask the executor's permission to let Patrick know.

para 6.3 SRA Code of Conduct for Solicitors deals with confidentiality. It states: *You keep the affairs of clients and former clients confidential unless disclosure is required or permitted by law or the client consents.* There are various statutes which allow certain government agencies, such as HM Revenue & Customs, to require law firms to disclose information **without** the client's consent – these exceptions are *permitted by law*.

Principle 7 should have been considered by Megan (above). Acting in the best interests of her client, Fiona, would include keeping her status as executor secret. Although Patrick's statement that he will know soon enough when probate is obtained (and the will is made public) was correct, Megan should have resisted her understandable wish to be helpful to a bereaved family member.

3.4.2.6 Duties owed to the court

para 1.4 and paras 2.1–2.7 SRA Code of Conduct for Solicitors concern how a lawyer should deal with ethical issues when faced with conflicting pressures from the client and a court. In addition, **Principle 1** requires that you act in a way that upholds the constitutional principle of the rule of law and the proper administration of justice.

para 1.4 states: *You do not mislead or attempt to mislead your clients, the court or others, either by your own acts or omissions or allowing or being complicit in the acts or omissions of others (including your client).*

para 2.1 states: *You do not misuse or tamper with evidence or attempt to do so.*

para 2.4 states: *You only make assertions or put forward statements, representations or submissions to the court or others which are properly arguable.* Where a client has admitted their guilt in a criminal offence to you, you must not argue their innocence in court.

para 2.5 requires you not to place yourself in contempt of court and **para 2.6** states that you must not waste the court's time.

para 2.7 states that you must draw the court's attention to relevant cases and statutory references which are likely to have a material effect on the case.

Consider the following examples.

(1) Annette's client, Ivan, admits to her that he carried out the assault with which he has been charged. He decides to plead not guilty and asks her to use an alibi witness in his defence.

(2) Kamal's client, Maxwell, has been arrested and charged with speeding. He admits the offence to Kamal and asks him to

try and persuade the Magistrates' Court not to disqualify him from driving. He will lose his job as a delivery van driver if he loses his licence.

What should Annette and Kamal do?

(1) Annette should refuse to act for Ivan. She does **not** have an obligation to disclose Ivan's admission to the court. Ivan can instruct a new lawyer to argue his case.

(2) If Maxwell is prepared to plead guilty to the offence, Kamal **will** be able to make a "plea in mitigation" requesting the court to allow Maxwell to keep his licence because he needs it for his job.

In-house lawyers must also comply with this rule and may need to explain to their employer, diplomatically but firmly, their professional obligations.

Activity!

A third of in-house lawyers placed in difficult moral positions

Read the following Law Society *Gazette* article (including the comments below it) https://www.lawgazette.co.uk/news/a-third-of-in-house-lawyers-placed-in-difficult-moral-positions-study-finds/5101966.article .

What examples are given of ethical issues where in-house lawyers have had to be prepared to be unpopular?

3.4.2.7 Duties owed to third parties

para 1.2 SRA Code of Conduct for Solicitors states that you should not take *unfair advantage of clients or others.*

para 1.2 is important when dealing with a third party who is your client's opponent in litigation or the other party in a transaction (e.g. a house sale). You should not contact the opponent or other party in person if they are already represented by a lawyer.

Increasing restrictions on access to legal aid have resulted in greater numbers of people representing themselves in court as "litigants in person". This causes significant difficulties for lawyers, judges and courtroom staff but you will be expected to make greater allowances for unrepresented opponents. In particular, you must not take unfair advantage of an unrepresented opponent's lack of legal knowledge.

3.4.3 Handling client data

Legal practice inevitably involves lawyers in the handling of personal data relating to clients – and indeed to others. The handling and use of personal data is regulated by the **UK General Data Protection Regulation** (**GDPR**) and the **Data Protection Act 2018**. Personal data is any data that relates to an identifiable individual.

There are different regulations to comply with depending on what you do with data. Most legal practices will be **controllers** of data. Controllers must comply with the data protection principles and other UK **GDPR** requirements. They must also register with the Information Commissioners Office (ICO) to notify them that they are using personal data.

The **GDPR** sets out seven key data protection principles which must be followed when processing personal data. Where personal data is held it must be:

- processed lawfully, fairly and transparently;
- processed for a specific purpose;

- limited to necessary data (i.e. you should not hold data that it is not needed);
- accurate;
- not kept for longer than necessary;
- kept securely; and
- controlled by someone who is accountable for that data and takes responsibility for complying with the other principles.

3.4.3.1 Cybersecurity

Cybersecurity is extremely important for law firms. Legal practices are attractive targets for cyber criminals, as they often hold both sensitive client data and large sums of client money. The consequences of a successful cyberattack can be devastating for clients, potentially including the loss of their home. The consequences for firms which fail to safeguard their clients' money and data from cyberattack can be correspondingly severe and firms can ultimately be shut down for such failures.

All legal practices need to take cybersecurity extremely seriously and take steps to mitigate the risks.

Activity!

Cyber threat to the UK Legal Sector

Read the National Cyber Security Centre's report: *Cyber Threat Report: UK Legal Sector* at https://www.ncsc.gov.uk/report/cyber-threat-report-uk-legal-sector .

Who are the main categories of individuals and groups targeting law firms? What are the main types of cyber-attack being used?

3.4.4 Financial crime

Law firms have been used by criminals to convert the cash proceeds of crime into legitimate investments, such as property. As a result, lawyers, together with other professionals such as accountants, are required by the **Money Laundering, Terrorist Financing and Transfer of Funds (Information on the Payer) Regulations 2017** and the **Proceeds of Crime Act 2002** to carry out certain identity checks before carrying out work for clients.

The money laundering legislation imposes a number of important requirements on law firms including a specific nomination of a money laundering reporting officer. As part of the checks which must be carried out, each client must provide identification such as a passport and a recent utility bill.

Activity!

Go to the SRA money-laundering webpage at https://www.sra.org.uk/solicitors/resources/money-laundering/what-does-my-firm-need-do/ .

What steps does a firm need to take to comply with the regulations?

3.4.5 Handling client money

Many areas of legal work require practitioners to look after significant sums on behalf of their clients. Examples include conveyancing where the proceeds of house sales may be hundreds of thousands of pounds and probate where valuable assets are cashed in pending distribution to the beneficiaries. Maintaining lawyers' reputations for financial honesty and integrity is vital. Both CILEX Regulation and the SRA have strict rules which govern the handling of client money.

The **CILEX Regulation Accounts Rules** and **SRA Accounts Rules** both require strict separation of clients' money from the firm's own cash. Essentially, whenever money is received by the firm on behalf of the client, it must be paid into the **client account**. The bureaucratic procedures for receiving and handling cheques and money transfers payable to clients will vary in different firms, but the rules laid down by the regulators must be met. You must learn the procedures applicable in your firm as soon as possible. Lawyers and support staff are able to monitor the sums in the client account using their firm's computer system and printouts. Interest is payable to clients in respect of money held on the client account.

When the firm submits a bill for its work (which may include expenses (disbursements)) **and** it has been approved by the client, the fee earner is able to transfer the sums concerned from the client account to the **office account**. The office account represents cash owned by the firm, and it must be kept strictly separate from the client account. If a cheque is received representing both client money and money to pay a bill, it must first be paid into the client account before the cash to pay the bill (assuming it has been approved) can be transferred.

Knowledge checks!

(1) Which of the following job roles does CILEX Regulation require firms which it regulates to appoint?

(a) Complaints Manager

(b) General Manager

(c) Compliance Manager

(d) Personnel Manager

(2) Which of the following statements about conflicts of interest applying to solicitors and their staff under the **SRA Code of Conduct for Solicitors** are correct?

(Select 2 correct answers)

(a) You should not act for a client if there is a significant risk of a conflict between the client's interest and your own personal interest.

(b) You should never act for two clients who have a conflict of interest.

(c) Acting for two clients who have a conflict of interest is permitted in all cases provided they have both consented.

(d) Acting for a mortgagor and a mortgagee purchasing a house is normally permitted.

(3) Herron LLP is a solicitors' firm which has received a bank transfer of £50,000 from a client to cover the cost of the deposit on a house purchase. Which account must the transfer be paid into?

(a) Office account

(b) Client account

(c) Conveyancing account

(4) Which job role must firms of solicitors and chartered legal executives have under the money laundering legislation?

(a) Money laundering reporting officer

(b) Money laundering regulation officer

(c) Money laundering prevention officer

3.5 Summary!

(1) Chartered legal executives are regulated by CILEX Regulation. CILEX Regulation also regulates legal practices run by chartered legal executive litigators and advocates, conveyancing practitioners, probate practitioners and immigration practitioners, as well as other "authorised persons" (including solicitors).

(2) Solicitors are regulated by the Solicitors Regulation Authority which sets out rules of professional conduct in the **SRA Code of Conduct for Solicitors**.

(3) Barristers are regulated by the Bar Standards Board.

(4) The Legal Services Board has overall responsibility for overseeing legal activities in England and Wales. It works with approved regulators.

(5) The Office for Legal Complaints supervises the Legal Ombudsman. The Legal Ombudsman is staffed by a chief ombudsman and three ombudsmen. It seeks to resolve complaints about lawyers informally but can award compensation of up to £50,000.

(6) Unless your firm is regulated by the Financial Conduct Authority, you will only be able to give investment advice if it falls within the **SRA Financial Services (Scope) Rules**.

(7) Lawyers regulated by the **CILEX Code of Conduct** or the **SRA Code of Conduct for Solicitors** have personal responsibility for ensuring they comply with regulatory requirements.

(8) The **SRA Code of Conduct for Solicitors** sets out seven mandatory principles which must be upheld in relation to all issues of professional ethics. These include obligations to maintain trust of clients and act fairly towards them and to ensure you are competent to undertake the work instructed.

(9) Conflicts of interest occur where either the lawyer (or their firm's) personal interests conflict with those of a client or where the interests of two clients cannot be protected because of the knowledge of the lawyer. In some cases, the lawyer may have to refuse to continue to act for both clients.

(10) It is vital to maintain the duty of confidentiality owed to clients including their personal details.

(11) All legal practices must comply with the UK **GDPR** principles on the handling of personal data.

(12) Law firms and their staff must comply with the **Money Laundering, Terrorist Financing and Transfer of Funds (Information on the Payer) Regulations 2017** and the **Proceeds of Crime Act 2002**. Customer due diligence must be applied and appropriate action taken when suspicious transactions occur.

(13) It is important to understand the rules governing the handling of client money under the **CILEX Regulation Account Rules** and **SRA Account Rules**. Clients' money must be kept separate in a client account and only transferred to the firm's office account when an invoice has been authorised.

CHAPTER **4**

Human rights and equality

4.1 Introduction
4.2 The European Convention on Human Rights
4.3 The Human Rights Act 1998
4.4 Protecting equality: Equality Act 2010
4.5 Summary!

Aims of chapter!

This chapter will enable you to:

- Explain the concept of civil liberties under the common law
- Distinguish between absolute, limited and qualified rights under the
- **European Convention on Human Rights**
- Explain the key articles of the **European Convention on Human Rights**
- Explain the significance of the **Human Rights Act 1998**
- Outline the key sections of the **Human Rights Act 1998**

- Explain how UK courts interpret the articles of the **European Convention on Human Rights** under **s2 HRA 1998**
- Explain the significance of the statement of compatibility under **s19 HRA 1998**
- Describe how UK courts interpret UK Acts and secondary legislation in the light of the **European Convention on Human Rights**
- Describe the significance of declarations of incompatibility
- Explain how public authorities are required to comply with the **European Convention on Human Rights**
- Describe how the **Police and Criminal Evidence Act 1984** provides
- Describe the protected characteristics under the **Equality Act 2010**
- Explain prohibited conduct under the **Equality Act 2010**: direct discrimination, indirect discrimination, harassment and victimisation, and
- Outline the role of the Equality and Human Rights Commission.

4.1 Introduction

This chapter examines the protection of human rights and equality within England and Wales. The key instruments for human rights protection in the UK are the **European Convention on Human Rights** (**ECHR**) and the **Human Rights Act 1998** (**HRA 1998**). **HRA 1998** incorporates **ECHR** into UK law. The chapter starts by examining the rights protected by **ECHR**, and how the law protects them through **HRA 1998**. The final sections of the chapter examine the particular human rights implications of the powers of the police and the protection of equality under the **Equality Act 2010**.

4.2 The European Convention on Human Rights

ECHR was established in the aftermath of the Second World War. Like the **United Nations' Universal Declaration of Human Rights 1948**, it was conceived as a mechanism for preventing a recurrence of the human rights abuses which occurred under fascist governments before and during the Second World War. Signatory states promise to secure the specified rights for their citizens.

ECHR sets out a list (by way of numbered articles) of individual human rights. Most may be subject to lawful restriction. In any event, the individual has to prove breach in order to gain a remedy. Rights have been added to the original treaty list, keeping it up to date with changing values. This is done by means of numbered protocols (somewhat unhelpfully sub-numbered by articles).

The United Kingdom was an original signatory to (and, indeed, played a major part in drafting) **ECHR** and recognises it in international law, and a UK citizen has (since the 1960s) been able to petition to the European Court of Human Rights (ECtHR). Since **HRA 1998**, nearly all of the rights in **ECHR** can be enforced in UK courts, so this is where actions are now brought and decided, although UK citizens may still go on to petition to the ECtHR if they have been unsuccessful in the UK courts.

Activity!

Watch the following video at: https://www. https://www.echr.coe.int/videos?p_l_back_url=%2Fsearch%3Fq%3Dfilm%2Bon%2Bthe%2Bcourt .

What were the facts of this case and what was the decision of the European Court of Human Rights?

4.2.1 The scope of ECHR rights

The key Articles of the Convention are set out below. It is important to pay close attention to the precise wording of each. The articles fall into three groups.

The first group is **absolute** rights (**Arts 3, 4** and **7**). These are absolute in terms (there are no exceptions in the text) but that does not mean they are entirely straightforward. The court must still interpret the scope of the text.

The second group is **limited** rights (**Arts 2, 5** and **6**). These contain narrow express exceptions or qualifications in the text of the articles themselves. As with absolute rights, that text will fall to be interpreted by the court.

The final group may be termed **qualified** rights (**Arts 8–12** and **Art 1 Protocol 1**). These are structured differently from limited rights and are more broadly drawn. **Articles 8–11** in particular follow a common structure, as they each contain two paragraphs, the first setting out the right and the second the conditions under which that right may be lawfully restricted.

The task for the court is thus arguably more complex in relation to these articles, for it must determine not only the scope of the rights under the first paragraph, but the scope of the lawful restriction of that right.

In determining whether an interference with one of the limited rights has been lawful, courts use the principle of **proportionality**. Proportionality is concerned with achieving a balance between two competing values or objectives. In the human rights context, that means a balance between (1) the rights of the individual and (2) any public interest which the government may have in overriding that right.

4.2.2 The right to life

Article 2:

(1) *Everyone's right to life shall be protected by law. No one shall be deprived of his life intentionally save in the execution of a sentence of a court following his conviction of a crime for which this penalty is provided by law.*

(2) *Deprivation of life shall not be regarded as inflicted in contravention of this Article when it results from the use of force which is no more than absolutely necessary:*

(a) *in defence of any person from unlawful violence;*

(b) *in order to effect a lawful arrest or to prevent escape of a person law- fully detained;*

(c) *in action lawfully taken for the purpose of quelling a riot or insurrection.*

Two things should be noted about **Art 2** at the outset. First, the right to life is expressly qualified, that is a death resulting from state action or inaction may be lawful. That said, the words "shall be protected" emphasise a state duty. Second, that **Art 2** must be read in conjunction with **Article 1 Protocol 13** which expressly prohibits capital punishment, effectively making the second sentence of the first paragraph redundant.

As well as the obligation not to deprive of life, **Art 2** imposes an obligation on the state to protect life. In ***Edwards v UK [2002]*** the deceased was killed by a cellmate, who was known to be violent and unstable, while in police custody. The ECtHR held that the police had failed to protect the deceased's right to life.

NB There is no right to die under **Art 2** – see https://www.equalityhumanrights.com/human-rights/human-rights-act/article-2-right-life .

4.2.3 The prohibition of torture, inhuman or degrading treatment or punishment

Article 3:

> *No one shall be subjected to torture or to inhuman or degrading treatment or punishment.*

The prohibition upon torture, inhuman or degrading treatment or punishment is in terms absolute: it has no qualifications and cannot be subject to lawful restriction. However, the provisions still require interpretation.

Like **Art 2**, **Art 3** imposes positive obligations on the state to protect individuals from torture and inhuman or degrading treatment. In ***DSD and Another v Commissioner of the Police for the Metropolis [2014]*** it was found that the defendants, the Metropolitan Police, were liable for breach of **Art 3** as a result of "systemic failings" in the investigative processes in the "Black Cab Rapist" case. John Worboys had been convicted of over 100 charges of rape and sexual assault in 2009.

4.2.4 The prohibition on slavery

Article 4:

> *(1) No one shall be held in slavery or servitude.*
>
> *(2) No one shall be required to perform forced or compulsory labour.*

Like **Art 3**, **Art 4** is absolute: there are no permitted exceptions. Cases on **Art 4** are relatively rare, but do arise, particularly in relation to human trafficking. In ***CN v United Kingdom [2012]*** the applicant was a Ugandan national who had been helped to enter the UK lawfully and then had her passport and visa removed by a relative. She was required to work full-time as a carer and never received wages. She eventually contacted the police and claimed asylum, but her claim was refused and the police investigation was stopped. The ECtHR held that the UK had breached **Art 4** in failing to adopt specific legislation criminalising slavery. This gap was remedied by **s71 Coroners and Justice Act 2009**, and subsequently the **Modern Slavery Act 2015**.

4.2.5 The right to liberty and security of person

Article 5:

(1) Everyone has the right to liberty and security of person. No one shall be deprived of his liberty save in the following cases and in accordance with a procedure prescribed by law:

(a) the lawful detention of a person after conviction by a competent court;

(b) the lawful arrest or detention of a person for non-compliance with the lawful order of a court in order to secure the fulfilment of any obligation prescribed by law;

(c) the lawful arrest or detention of a person effected for the purpose of bringing him before the competent legal authority, on reasonable suspicion of having committed an offence or when it is reasonably considered necessary to prevent his committing an offence or fleeing after having done so;

(d) the detention of a minor by lawful order for the purpose of educational supervision or his lawful detention for the purpose of bringing him before the competent legal authority;

(e) the lawful detention of persons for the prevention of the spreading of infectious diseases, of persons of unsound mind, alcoholics or drug addicts or vagrants;

(f) the lawful arrest or detention of a person to prevent his effecting an unauthorised entry into the country or of a person against whom action is being taken with a view to deportation or extradition.

(2) *Everyone who is arrested shall be informed promptly, in a language which he understands, of the reasons for his arrest and of any charge against him.*

(3) *Everyone arrested or detained in accordance with the provisions of para 1(c) of this Article shall be brought promptly before a judge or other officer authorised by law to exercise judicial power, and shall be entitled to trial within a reasonable time or to release pending trial. Release may be conditioned by guarantees to appear for trial.*

(4) *Everyone who is deprived of his liberty by arrest or detention shall be entitled to take proceedings by which the lawfulness of his detention shall be decided speedily by a court and his release ordered if the detention is not lawful.*

(5) *Everyone who has been the victim of arrest or detention in contravention of the provisions of this Article shall have an enforceable right to compensation.*

Art 5 falls into two parts. The first paragraph sets out the right to liberty and security of the person, subject to six clearly stated exceptions. Paragraphs two to five then set out procedural safeguards which apply when a person is deprived of their liberty.

Most of the case law on **Art 5** is concerned with the question of when a person will be held to have been deprived of their liberty. In ***Austin v Metropolitan Police Commissioner [2009]*** the House of Lords held that demonstrators who had been confined within a police cordon for several hours (a practice known as "kettling") did not suffer a violation of their right to liberty guaranteed by **Art 5** if the cordon was part of the crowd control measures adopted by the police in order to prevent a breach of public order, and the measures were not arbitrary but were resorted to in good faith, were proportionate and were enforced for no longer than was reasonably necessary.

4.2.6 The right to a fair trial

Article 6:

(1) In the determination of his civil rights and obligations or of any criminal charge against him, everyone is entitled to a fair and public hearing within a reasonable time by an independent and impartial tribunal established by law. Judgment shall be pronounced publicly but the press and public may be excluded from all or part of the trial in the interest of morals, public order or national security in a democratic society, where the interests of juveniles or the protection of the private life of the parties so require, or to the extent strictly necessary in the opinion of the court in special circumstances where publicity would prejudice the interests of justice.

(2) Everyone charged with a criminal offence shall be presumed innocent until proved guilty according to law.

(3) Everyone charged with a criminal offence has the following minimum rights:

(a) to be informed promptly, in a language which he understands and in detail, of the nature and cause of the accusation against him;

(b) to have adequate time and facilities for the preparation of his defence;

(c) to defend himself in person or through legal assistance of his own choosing or, if he has not sufficient means to pay for legal assistance, to be given it free when the interests of justice so require;

(d) to examine or have examined witnesses against him and to obtain the attendance and examination of witnesses on his behalf under the same conditions as witnesses against him;

(e) to have the free assistance of an interpreter if he cannot understand or speak the language used in court.

Art 6 is one of the rights most commonly raised in litigation. Note that while paragraph 1 applies in all proceedings, paragraphs 2 and 3 apply only in criminal proceedings.

In ***Golder v United Kingdom [1975]*** Golder, a prisoner, wished to take civil action. He was refused permission to write to a solicitor. This was a breach of **Art 6** as it denied access to the courts. It was also a breach of **Art 8** (respect for correspondence).

4.2.7 The prohibition of punishment for retrospective crimes

Article 7:

> *(1) No one shall be held guilty of any criminal offence on account of any act or omission which did not constitute a criminal offence under national or international law at the time when it was committed. Nor shall a heavier penalty be imposed than the one that was applicable at the time the criminal offence was committed.*
>
> *(2) This Article shall not prejudice the trial and punishment of any person for any act or omission which, at the time when it was committed, was criminal according to the general principles of law recognised by civilised nations.*

Art 7 has not often been litigated, but an example is found in ***SW v United Kingdom; CR v United Kingdom [1996]***. Here the applicants had been convicted of raping their wives. Until the decision of the House of Lords in ***R v R [1991]***, it had not been generally understood that rape could take place within marriage. The applicants complained that the common law, by imposing criminal liability for actions which, at the time they had been committed, were not criminal, was in breach of **Art 7**. The ECtHR rejected the contention, on the basis that **Art 7** did not forbid the gradual clarification of the principles of criminal liability on a case-by-case basis, provided that the development could be reasonably foreseen.

4.2.8 The right to respect for private and family life

Article 8:

(1) Everyone has the right to respect for his private and family life, his home and his correspondence.

(2) There shall be no interference by a public authority with the exercise of this right except such as is in accordance with the law and is necessary in a democratic society in the interests of national security, public safety or the economic well-being of the country, for the prevention of disorder or crime, for the protection of health or morals, or for the protection of the rights and freedom of others.

Art 8 is, in terms of its case law, probably the most complex article of **ECHR**. The ECtHR has teased out distinct rights of private life, family life, the right to respect for one's home, and the right to respect for one's correspondence.

The concept of the right to privacy is itself a broad one. At its heart is that the individual should be free from interferences with their physical and psychological integrity. Thus, in ***Gillan and Quinton v United Kingdom [2010]*** the ECtHR held that use of stop and search powers without proper safeguards breached **Art 8**.

Art 8 has been applied to the dissemination of images, and particularly information about individuals. This has been particularly problematic in relation to public figures, who may have their private information and images published in the media. As such, this area may require the court to weigh the balance between an individual's right to privacy under **Art 8**, against freedom of expression rights under **Art 10**. In the UK context, this has led to the development, in ***Campbell v Mirror Group Newspapers [2004]***, of the tort of misuse of private information. In this case the model Naomi Campbell successfully took action against a newspaper group for publishing a story about her drug addiction and treatment.

4.2.9 The right to freedom of thought, conscience and religion

Article 9:

> (1) *Everyone has the right to freedom of thought, conscience and religion; this right includes freedom to change his religion or belief, and freedom, either alone or in community with others and in public or private, to manifest his religion or belief, in worship, teaching, practice and observance.*
>
> (2) *Freedom to manifest one's religion or beliefs shall be subject only to such limitations as are prescribed by law and are necessary in a democratic society in the interests of public safety, for the protection of public order, health or morals, or for the protection of the rights and freedoms of others.*

Art 9 contains two distinct elements: first, the right to hold a belief; and second, the right to manifest it (make it public). The ECtHR takes a broad approach to what amounts to religion or belief, the definition of which includes druidism (***Chappell v United Kingdom [1989]***), pacifism (***Arrowsmith v United Kingdom [1978]***) and veganism (***H v United Kingdom [1993]***).

The majority of the case law on **Art 9** concerns the right to manifest beliefs. In ***Eweida and Others v UK [2013]*** the ECtHR issued its ruling in four cases concerning Christians from various denominations being disciplined by their employer, or even losing their jobs, for manifesting their faith: wearing a small cross on a chain around their neck in the cases of Eweida and Chaplin and refusing to register a same-sex partnership (in the case of Ladele). In the case of McFarlane, a marriage counsellor, he was dismissed after sharing with his superiors his moral doubts as to his personal ability to counsel same-sex couples. The only victory of the four was won by Eweida. In the case of Chaplin, the court said that the hospital which employed her was right to refuse to let her wear a cross on a chain over her nurse's uniform as it posed a hazard to health and safety. The judges found that in the cases of Ladele and McFarlane, the sanctions imposed by their respective employers were justified and fell within the wide discretion they could exercise in applying the law.

4.2.10 The right to freedom of expression

Article 10:

(1) *Everyone has the right to freedom of expression. This right shall include freedom to hold opinions and to receive and impart information and ideas without interference by public authority and regardless of frontiers. This Article shall not prevent States from requiring the licensing of broadcasting, television or cinema enterprises.*

(2) *The exercise of these freedoms, since it carries with it duties and responsibilities, may be subject to such formalities, conditions, restrictions or penalties as are prescribed by law and are necessary in a democratic society, in the interests of national security, territorial integrity or public safety, for the prevention of disorder or crime, for the protection of health or morals, for the protection of the reputation or rights of others, for preventing the disclosure of information received in confidence, or for maintaining the authority and impartiality of the judiciary.*

Expression within **Art 10** has a broad meaning, embracing not only written and spoken words (expressed, e.g. in the street, in public addresses, through books and the media), but also other forms such as flags, banners and art.

In general, the ECtHR places particularly high value (and accordingly affords a high level of protection for) political speech, as a key element of a functioning democracy. Accordingly, press freedom, in relation to matters of public interest, is afforded a high degree of protection. In ***Goodwin v United Kingdom [2002]***, the ECtHR held that an order for disclosure of a journalist's source was a breach of **Art 10**.

A much lower value (and lower protection) is afforded for artistic or commercial expression. In ***Muller v Switzerland [1991]*** the applicant was a painter who was convicted and fined for publishing obscene material. The ECtHR held that **Art 10** had not been breached: the conviction by the Swiss court was not unreasonable.

4.2.11 Freedom of assembly and of peaceful association

Article 11:

(1) Everyone has the right to freedom of peaceful assembly and the freedom of association with others, including the right to form and to join trade unions for the protection of his interests.

(2) No restrictions shall be placed on the exercise of these rights other than such as are prescribed by law and are necessary in a democratic society in the interests of national security or public safety, for the prevention of disorder or crime, for the protection of health or morals or for the protection of the rights and freedoms of others...

"Assembly" refers to the typical public protest in Hyde Park or a public meeting in a village hall. "Association" refers to freedom to join organisations such as political parties or trade unions.

In ***Young, James and Webster v United Kingdom [1981]*** the applicants had been dismissed for refusing to join a trade union. British Rail had a "closed shop" agreement that specified which unions employees could join. It was held that **Art 11** implies that everyone has the freedom to choose which union they join, as well as the right **not** to join a union. This freedom had been denied to the applicants.

4.2.12 The right to marry and found a family

Article 12:

Men and women of marriageable age have the right to marry and to found a family, according to the national laws governing the exercise of this right.

Whilst the institution of marriage retains protective recognition, as values have changed since **ECHR** was drafted in 1950, the interpretation of **ECHR** has adapted accordingly.

The ECtHR held in ***B v United Kingdom [2005]*** that the **Marriage Act 1949** prohibiting the marriage of a father-in-law to a daughter-in-law violated the right to marry. The **Marriage Act 1949** was amended accordingly. The **Civil Partnership Act 2004** enables same-sex couples to obtain legal recognition of their relationship by registering a civil partnership. Same-sex marriages are now permitted under the **Marriage (Same Sex Couples) Act 2013**.

4.2.13 The prohibition of discrimination

Article 14:

> *The enjoyment of the rights and freedoms set forth in this Convention shall be secured without discrimination on any ground such as sex, race, colour, language, religion, political or other opinion, national or social origin, association with a national minority, property, birth or other status.*

Art 14 is unusual in that it cannot be relied upon independently. **Art 14** is "parasitic" upon breach of other articles: the applicant must demonstrate that they have suffered discrimination in relation to their enjoyment of another substantive right.

In ***Re an Application by Siobhan McLaughlin for Judicial Review (Child Poverty Action Group and another intervening) [2018]*** the Supreme Court considered the claim by an unmarried partner for widowed parent's allowance following the death of her partner. The applicant and her partner had a relationship lasting 23 years and had four children. Widowed parent's allowance is a contributory, non-means-tested, social security benefit payable to men and women with dependent children, who were widowed before March 2017. Under **s39A Social Security**

Contributions and Benefits (Northern Ireland) Act 1992 the widowed parent can claim the allowance only if he or she was married to or the civil partner of the deceased. The applicant argued that **s39A** was discriminatory against herself and her children under **Art 14 ECHR** when read with **Art 8** (respect for private and family life) and **Art 1 Protocol 1** (right to peaceful enjoyment of possessions). The Supreme Court held in favour of the applicant.

Lady Hale found that the circumstances were clearly within the ambit of both **Art 8** and **Art 1 Protocol 1** and there was a clear difference between the treatment of the applicant and her children from the treatment she would have received if she had been married. It was clear that the difference of treatment was because of "other status" (being an unmarried partner). While the protection of marriage was a legitimate aim, the denial of the benefit to Ms McLaughlin was not a proportionate means of achieving that aim. The purpose of the allowance was to diminish the financial loss caused to families with children by the death of a parent and this loss was not diminished by parents being unmarried.

4.2.14 Derogation from Convention rights

Art 15 is unusual. It provides not a substantive right, but a mechanism by which rights may be disapplied in certain circumstances.

Article 15:

> *(1) In time of war or other public emergency threatening the life of the nation any High Contracting Party may take measures derogating from its obligations under this Convention to the extent strictly required by the exigencies of the situation, provided that such measures are not inconsistent with its other obligations under international law.*
>
> *(2) No derogation from Article 2 except in respect of deaths resulting from lawful acts of war, or from Articles 3, 4 (paragraph 1) and 7 shall be made under this provision.*

(3) Any High Contracting Party availing itself of this right of derogation shall keep the Secretary-General of the Council of Europe fully informed of the measures which it has taken and the reasons therefor. It shall also inform the Secretary-General of the Council of Europe when such measures have ceased to operate and the provisions of the Convention are again fully executed.

The UK government attempted to derogate from **Art 5** in relation to provisions of the **Anti-Terrorism, Crime and Security Act 2001**. These provisions allowed the indefinite detention without charge of those certified as international terrorists. In ***A v Secretary of State for the Home Department [2004]*** the House of Lords held that the derogation was not *"to the extent strictly required by the exigencies of the situation"* as required by **Art 15 para 1**. Consequently, the derogation order was invalid and the House of Lords issued a declaration of incompatibility in relation to the relevant provisions of the **Anti-Terrorism, Crime and Security Act 2001**.

4.3 The Human Rights Act 1998

4.3.1 The background to incorporation

Until **HRA 1998** came into force in 2000, UK citizens who alleged breaches of their human rights under **ECHR** had to go to the ECtHR. This was expensive and increasingly time-consuming, as more European states signed **ECHR** and increased its workload, and as the ECtHR's case law became more nuanced and complex.

The objective of **HRA 1998** was "bringing rights home". In effect, UK courts were able, for the first time, to apply the legal rights in **ECHR** directly to UK cases. Only if a case had progressed through the UK courts could it now be considered by the ECtHR.

4.3.2 The structure and key features of the Human Rights Act 1998

HRA 1998 has an impact across the whole legal system. It protects rights in two key ways.

First, it tries to ensure that legislation is made and interpreted in line with **ECHR** rights. It does this through three key sections:

- **s19** aims to ensure that all new legislation which is made complies with **ECHR** rights.
- **s3** requires all legislation to be interpreted in line with **ECHR** rights so far as possible.
- **s4** allows a **declaration of incompatibility** to be made if primary legislation cannot be interpreted in a way which is compatible with **ECHR** rights under **s3**.

Second, **HRA 1998** requires that public authorities act in a **ECHR**-compatible way and provides mechanisms for individuals to make legal challenges if they do not:

- **s6** states that it is unlawful for a public authority to act in a manner which is incompatible with **ECHR** rights.
- **s7** allows a person who is a victim of a breach of **ECHR** rights to bring pro- ceedings against a public authority or rely on the **ECHR** right in proceedings involving a public authority.
- **s8** allows for the provision of a remedy, where **ECHR** rights have been breached.

4.3.3 The interpretation of Convention rights

s2 is concerned with the interpretation of **ECHR** rights themselves, that is, the meaning of the Articles of the Convention discussed at **10.3.2** and following. **s2** is potentially relevant in any case which concerns **ECHR** rights, though in practice, the interpretation of individual **ECHR** rights will not be controversial in most cases.

s2(1) provides:

A court or tribunal determining a question which has arisen in connection with a Convention right must take into account any:

- *(a) judgment, decision, declaration or advisory opinion of the European Court of Human Rights;*
- *(b) opinion of the Commission given in a report adopted under Article 31 of the Convention;*
- *(c) decision of the Commission in connection with Article 26 or 27(2) of the Convention; or*
- *(d) decision of the Committee of Ministers taken under Article 46 of the Convention,*

whenever made or given, so far as, in the opinion of the court or tribunal, it is relevant to the proceedings in which that question has arisen.

s2 requires then that a court, faced with an issue of interpretation of the Articles of the **ECHR**, must *take into account* (amongst other things) the judgments of the ECtHR. The key element in the provision is *take into account*. It does not say that UK courts are bound by decisions of the ECtHR, or that decisions of the ECtHR **must** be followed.

In practice, the UK courts will usually follow decisions of the ECtHR. In ***R (Ullah) v Special Adjudicator [2004]*** Lord Bingham set out what has come to be known as the "mirror principle", stating that:

> *"The duty of national courts is to keep pace with the Strasbourg* jurisprudence as it evolves over time: no more, but certainly no less".*
>
> *The European Court of Human Rights is based in Strasbourg.

4.3.4 s19 and the statement of compatibility

s19 HRA 1998 provides as follows:

> (1) *A Minister of the Crown in charge of a Bill in either House of Parliament must, before Second Reading of the Bill—*
>
> (a) *make a statement to the effect that in his view the provisions of the Bill are compatible with the Convention rights ("a statement of compatibil- ity"); or*
>
> (b) *make a statement to the effect that although he is unable to make a statement of compatibility the government nevertheless wishes the House to proceed with the Bill.*

The section requires a minister sponsoring new legislation to make a statement to Parliament that that Bill is compatible with **ECHR**. It serves to focus MPs' minds on the human rights implications of proposed legislation. Parliament is not, however, prevented from making legislation which does not comply with **ECHR**: **s19(1)(b)** makes explicit provision for that.

4.3.5 s3 and the interpretation of legislation

s3 provides as follows:

> (1) *So far as it is possible to do so, primary legislation and subordinate legislation must be read and given effect in a way which is compatible with the Convention rights.*
>
> (2) *This section—*
>
> (a) *applies to primary legislation and subordinate legislation whenever enacted;*

> (b) *does not affect the validity, continuing operation or enforcement of any incompatible primary legislation; and*
>
> (c) *does not affect the validity, continuing operation or enforcement of any incompatible subordinate legislation if (disregarding any possibility of revocation) primary legislation prevents removal of the incompatibility.*

s3 requires courts to interpret primary legislation in line with **ECHR** rights *so far as it is possible to do so*. Essentially, **HRA 1998** introduced a new power and method of statutory interpretation.

4.3.6 s4: the declaration of incompatibility

s4(2) states:

> (2) *If the court is satisfied that the provision is incompatible with a Convention right, it may make a declaration of that incompatibility.*

A declaration of incompatibility is a statement that a particular statutory provision does **not** comply with a **ECHR** right. It has no impact on the validity or enforceability of the legislation (as is clear from **s4(6)(a)**): UK courts cannot "quash" (annul) primary legislation (Acts of Parliament). Secondary legislation may, however, be quashed if incompatible with **ECHR**.

Note that a declaration of incompatibility is not binding on the parties to the case in which it is made (**s4(6)(b)**).

The function of a declaration of incompatibility is to highlight the incompatibility. In so doing, it places pressure on the government to change the law to remove the incompatibility. This is usually successful: most declarations of incompatibility are ultimately resolved, either through primary legislation, or occasionally through the use of the remedial powers found in **s10**. **s10** allows a minister, where a declaration of incompatibility has been made, to introduce secondary legislation to remove an incompatibility with **ECHR** in primary legislation.

The Ministry of Justice publishes an annual report into declarations of incompatibility (and any findings in the ECtHR against the UK) and how the government has responded to them. The most recent report may be found at https://www.gov.uk/government/publications/responding-to-human-rights-judgments-2022-to-2023 .

Activity!

Read the press summary of the Supreme Court decision in ***R (on the application of Steinfeld and Keidan) (Appellants) v Secretary of State for International Development [2018]*** at https://www.supremecourt.uk/cases/uksc-2017-0060.html .

Summarise the facts of this case.

What was the court's decision in relation to a declaration of incompatibility?

4.3.7 s6: unlawful acts of public authorities

s6 provides:

> *(1) It is unlawful for a public authority to act in a way which is incompatible with a Convention right.*

What is a public authority?

The definition of "public authority" is found in **s6(3)**:

> *(3) … "public authority" includes –*
>
> *(a) a court or tribunal, and*

> (b) *any person certain of whose functions are functions of a public nature,*
>
> *but does not include either House of Parliament or a person exercising functions in connection with proceedings in Parliament.*

The definition of public authority was considered by the House of Lords decision in ***YL v Birmingham City Council [2008]***: was the defendant, a private care home which had residents whose care was paid for by the local authority, a public authority for the purposes of **s6**? The House of Lords held that the key question was why the body was providing this function. The answer was that it was a commercial business carrying out activities for profit. It should not be considered a public authority, even though the care home was subject to a great deal of regulation and received public funding.

4.3.8 s7: bringing proceedings to the court

The key provision for understanding when **s6** can be used before the court is **s7**, which provides:

> (1) *A person who claims that a public authority has acted (or proposes to act) in a way which is made unlawful by **s6(1)** may—*
>
> (a) *bring proceedings against the authority under this Act in the appropriate court or tribunal, or*
>
> (b) *rely on the Convention right or rights concerned in any legal proceedings, but only if he is (or would be) a victim of the unlawful act.*

s7 introduces two routes to using **s6**. First, it can be used to bring proceedings under **s7(1)(a)**. However, **s7(1)(b)** says that **ECHR** rights can be used in **any** legal proceedings. This means that **ECHR** arguments can be brought into any other case if relevant.

Key to **s7** is that it can only be used by a **victim** of the unlawful act. (***Attorney-General (Rusbridger) [2003]***).

4.3.9 Remedies

s8 HRA 1998 addresses remedies. Under **s8(1)** all common law remedies which the court views as appropriate are available. The normal remedy will be damages.

4.4 Protecting equality: Equality Act 2010

The **European Convention on Human Rights** and **Human Rights Act 1998** provide some protection against discrimination, but do not provide a comprehensive or systematic approach to this. The UK has separate legislation on equality, the **Equality Act 2010**, which protects against discrimination and other forms of unlawful conduct.

4.4.1 The framework of the Equality Act 2010

The **Equality Act 2010** (**EA 2010**) replaced a number of previous anti-discrimination laws with a single Act, unifying anti-discrimination law into a single framework.

EA 2010 establishes a framework of **protected characteristics** and **prohibited conduct**. Under **EA 2010** it is unlawful to discriminate against someone (or act in another manner that is prohibited) because of a protected characteristic. **EA 2010** protects people when using public services (such as accessing healthcare); at work; in education; when using goods or services (such as in restaurants or shops); when using transport; and when joining a club or association.

4.4.2 Protected characteristics

EA 2010 covers nine protected characteristics, which cannot be used as a reason to treat people unfairly. The protected characteristics are:

- age;
- disability;
- gender reassignment;
- marriage and civil partnership;
- pregnancy and maternity;
- race;
- religion or belief;
- sex; and
- sexual orientation.

The protections afforded to the different characteristics are not precisely the same. There are specific provisions relating to certain characteristics in particular situations: for example, there are detailed provisions addressing sex equality in the workplace and access to transport for disabled persons. There are also exemptions from the general provisions in certain circumstances. For example, it is lawful to provide single sex hospital wards.

4.4.3 Prohibited conduct

EA 2010 sets out the different ways in which it is unlawful to treat someone. There are five main forms of prohibited conduct: direct discrimination, indirect discrimination, associative direct discrimination, harassment and victimisation.

Direct discrimination is where person A treats person B less favourably than person A would treat others, because B has a protected characteristic. For example, it would be unlawful to refuse person B a promotion because she is pregnant.

Associative direct discrimination arises where someone is treated unfairly because a person they are associated with has a protected characteristic. An example would be where an employee is dismissed after marrying a Muslim.

Indirect discrimination is where person A adopts practices or policies which impact more severely on people (such as B) with a protected characteristic. For example, a company advertises a job requiring 10 years' experience. This could potentially be indirect discrimination on the basis of age, because it would exclude younger people who may still have the qualifications and skills necessary to do the job.

4.4.4 The Public Sector Equality Duty

s149 EA 2010 imposes a particular duty on public authorities in relation to equality, the Public Sector Equality Duty (PSED). Public authorities are to have due regard to the need to eliminate conduct prohibited under the Act; to advance equality of opportunity between persons who share and do not share a protected characteristic; and to foster good relations between persons who share a relevant protected characteristic. This means that public authorities must consider how their decisions affect people who are protected under **EA 2010**. The duty is legally enforceable.

4.4.5 The Equality and Human Rights Commission

The **Equality Act 2006** established the Equality and Human Rights Commission (EHRC) (see https://www.equalityhumanrights.com/). The commission has duties to promote equality and human rights and has a range of powers underpinning this, including the issuing of codes of practice, conducting inquiries and investigating whether persons have committed unlawful acts.

Some of the commission's work is broad ranging in nature: for example, the commission produced a range of guidance relating to the impact of the coronavirus pandemic on equality and human rights. Other work looks specifically at particular individuals or organisations: recent investigations by the commission have included the treatment of disabled benefits claimants by the Department for Work and Pensions and alleged discrimination at Pontins holiday camps.

Knowledge checks!

(1) Which of the following is **not** a protected characteristic under the **Equality Act 2010**?

(a) Gender orientation

(b) Age

(c) Disability

(d) Gender reassignment

(2) Match the following Articles of the **European Convention on Human Rights** with the relevant rights:

Art 2	Right to liberty and security of person
Art 5	Right to respect for private and family life
Art 8	Prohibition of discrimination
Art 14	Right to life

4.5 Summary!

(1) The **Human Rights Act 1998** incorporates the **European Convention on Human Rights** in the form of a schedule to the Act. UK courts can now apply the human rights listed in **ECHR** directly.

(2) **ECHR** provides for key individual rights, such as the right to life, freedom from torture, right to a fair trial, privacy, free speech, security of the person and freedom of assembly.

(3) **HRA 1998** provides two key routes to protecting rights: it seeks to ensure legislation complies with **ECHR** rights; and it requires public authorities to comply with **ECHR** rights.

(4) Under **s2 HRA 1998** courts are bound to take into account the case law of the ECtHR when determining cases involving **ECHR** rights.

(5) Under **s19(1)(a) HRA 1998**, when introducing a Bill to Parliament, the relevant minister must make a "statement of compatibility" confirming that the provisions of the Bill comply with **ECHR** rights. Alternatively, non-compliance with **ECHR** must be confirmed under **s19(1)(b)**.

(6) Under **s3 HRA 1998** legislation must, so far as is possible, be read and given effect to in a way which is compatible with **ECHR**.

(7) Where a higher court concludes that a provision in an Act of Parliament is incompatible with an **ECHR** right, it may, under **s4(1)**, grant a declaration of incompatibility to that effect. This does not invalidate the Act, but draws the attention of the government to the incompatibility.

(8) **s6 HRA 1998** makes it unlawful for a public authority to act in a way which is incompatible with **ECHR** rights.

(9) Only a victim of a violation of **ECHR** rights can raise the issue before the courts.

(10) A court can award remedies available at common law, including damages, though this is rare.

(11) The **Equality Act 2010** provides protection for nine protected characteristics: age; disability; gender reassignment; marriage and civil partnership; pregnancy and maternity; race; religion or belief; sex; and sexual orientation.

(12) The **Equality Act 2010** prohibits discrimination on the basis of one of the protected characteristics. It also prohibits harassment and victimisation on these bases.

(13) The Public Sector Equality Duty under **s149 Equality Act 2010** requires public authorities to consider how their decisions affect people who are protected under the **Equality Act 2010**.

(14) The Equality and Human Rights Commission is charged with promoting equality and human rights. It has a range of statutory powers to support this.

CHAPTER 5

The Client Relationship

Aims of chapter!

This chapter will help you to:

- Distinguish between external and internal clients
- Describe how to nurture relationships with clients
- Explain the requirements of acting ethically

5.1 Introduction

We tend to think of the client relationship as that of the traditional client-lawyer relationship. However, a client is anyone who is using legal services whether it is provided by a lawyer, another legal professional or a supporting business.

In this chapter we will identify how external clients, those outside the organisation, differ from internal clients, who are working within the organisation, differ. We will examine how these relationships can be developed and enhanced.

We will also consider how lawyers can nurture relationships with all types of clients. Finally, we will examine how lawyers should act ethically when working with clients.

5.2 The external client

External clients are relationships that exist outside of the business that contribute to the effectiveness and productivity of the business, therefore impacting on its success. By using a supply or service chain, the business is able to provide for successful case management without undertaking the overhead costs of complete involvement. This also means the business is able to "shop around" for more cost-effective providers or to seek a more efficient scope of work, leading to a strategic, goal focused organisation.

A service chain is defined as the entire process of creating, facilitating and delivering legal services to the consumer. A service chain focuses on key areas to maximise efficiency, quality of service and profitability. The legal firm assesses its strengths and weaknesses, identifies where value can be added and sets about achieving this through measurable objectives, and transferring work to external clients within their service chain who are more adept to complete it.

External clients come in three different forms with some examples listed below:

Form	Examples
They provide a stream of income	Private clients Business clients Banks and building societies Trade unions
They support the business	Counsel Medical agencies Medical experts
They provide outsourced services to the business	Legal expenses insurers Cost lawyers Lawyers who have specialisms outside those of your business

Maintaining successful relationships with external service chain clients is as important as managing the traditional client-lawyer relationship. Without outsourced services, the ability to progress a client's matter becomes problematic. In the first instance, without service chain relationships the firm may not be able to undertake the scope of work requested, finding themselves unsustainable in a legal landscape that is constantly evolving to meet the needs of the consumer and regulatory changes. Secondly, if legal businesses can diversity their proposition, they maintain independence whilst creating loyalty and reliability for the consumer.

By becoming strategic and developing strong resilient relationships with external clients, a business is able to define four dimensions that underpin its success.

- The business applies a strategic approach to business planning, identifying objectives and goals – this enables the service chain client to understand the organisation and how they fit into the "bigger picture" of success.

- By collaborating with external clients, the business opens opportunities to provide and receive feedback improving quality of service, reputation and profitability.
- The business has a clear governance structure – defining methods for communication, process, managing risk; measurements for success and failures.
- Improving communication and trust – building trust with an external client takes time and investment, often starting with small projects and as success is achieved, branching out into more significant work, whilst also developing tools and mechanisms to support processes.

A lawyer may sit anywhere in the service chain supporting the business. For example, they may be part of an Alternative Business Structure (ABS) providing legal services to a car insurance provider or they may be employed in the conveyancing sector by an organisation providing services investigating title. The lawyer may even be practising within a trade union organisation providing legal advice to members. In all of these scenarios the lawyer forms part of a service chain where each contributor relies on external relationships to achieve success.

Being able to understand the rules that govern the client-lawyer relationship is essential to understanding of the external client relationship and its influence. A lawyer has a duty to provide their client with appropriate legal advice that keeps them updated, enabling them to make informed decisions as to the timelines and fees incurred during the legal transaction. This includes disbursements that may be paid to third parties on their behalf to progress the matter or information disclosed to third parties for the same reason.

The most important or impactful external client relationship that exists is between the lawyer and the client. Learning how to develop trust and confidence within the client-lawyer relationship is key to the success of the organisation. In modern times, legal firms can no longer rely on the fact that customers will use their local high street firm for all of their legal services. With changes to legal funding, the consumer purchases increasingly on price and reputation. In terms of comparisons, the consumer will research a legal service in the same way as they would buy a new kitchen appliance or select a mobile phone provider. They expect legal services to be available no matter where they are located, they expect them to be reasonably priced and they will read reviews before deciding which firm to use for their requirement. Once a good relationship is established and a high quality service delivered, the consumer will return. Sadly, if the service is not good, they will invariably leave a negative review on social media to warn others. This can be hugely damaging for a business, not only to income, but also to the fee earners and those working internally, decreasing motivation and commitment.

Protecting the client's information is a guiding principle of the client-lawyer relationship. When dealing with external associated parties, the client must give express consent to disclosure of any information that is material to their case. The client must be made aware that the lawyer is sharing information, and must know what is being shared, with whom and why. There are only a few exceptions to this, such as when there is suspected fraud or regulatory investigation. Material information shared with external clients must only be disclosed to the extent of what is required to allow them to make an appropriate decision on the facts.

5.3 The internal client

Within a business there are a number of key relationships that allow the case to progress. In most firms and legal teams there will always be internal client relationships from other departments that work together to complete a task.

There are many examples of internal client relationships in a legal environment such as:

- accounts departments, teams that deal with client money and teams that deal with company money;

- internal quality assurance or audit teams;
- complaints departments;
- new business or first response teams;
- administration providers;
- IT support.

There are particular issues for in-house lawyers who have to advise other managers within the business. It can be challenging to stand up to the a non-lawyer who is also your employer and to advise them that a particular course of action is illegal.

Local authority legal teams need to advise not only other managers but elected councillors who may have strong political views and no awareness of the limitations of their legal powers.

5.4 Nurturing relationships

It is fundamental to nurture relationships internally and externally to achieve success.

The most important self-management tool that a lawyer must learn is how to manage expectations. By developing the skills to successfully manage expectations from the outset, a lawyer is the reassuring face of the relationship.

Managing expectations means the client understands from the outset what is their responsibility and what is the responsibility of the lawyer. A lawyer should not rely on the client's first point of contact to retrieve all of the salient information. The client welcomes the initial call with their lawyer and for you, it is the perfect opportunity to begin the relationship positively and with clarity.

There are simple and effective methods that a lawyer must utilise to manage client expectations.

- Find out exactly what the client's expectations are early on. We all want to make the client happy and our role easier, but even the best legal service will fail if the client's expectations are unrealistic. There is nothing worse than the client believing they are going to achieve a specific unrealistic goal because the lawyer did not take the time to have a challenging conversation early on in the relationship. In the initial discussions a lawyer must establish the requirement, the fees, their responsibilities, response times to communications and projected, realistic timelines.
- Remember, timelines are not static, they depend on external and internal factors. Lawyers should not make a promise to their client that they cannot guarantee and they must keep the client informed of any potential changes to timetables as soon as possible.
- The client must understand that the lawyer is there to provide appropriate legal advice including the risks and costs of pursuing unrealistic expectations. This can be difficult to discuss but will build trust and confidence with the client throughout the course of the case. Often the reason the client has approached the lawyer for representation is driven by emotion. The lawyer must be the voice of reason and provide practical advice that will help the client to achieve the best possible outcome for their case.
- The lawyer must make regular and meaningful contact with the client. It is important to keep the lines of communication open and revisit the initial goal to review if it is still the desired outcome. Understanding the problems and issues that arise is the responsibility of the lawyer; they are the expert. The client may need a process explained to them on the telephone and by email or letter. They will appreciate the time spent ensuring that they understand, in turn this nurtures trust, giving the client peace of mind and allowing the lawyer to easily discuss change or issues as the case progresses.
- Where there are problems, the lawyer should discuss solutions and avenues, being open and honest with the client. The client may feel

dejected, and anxious. They may lose focus and react emotionally. It is tempting to jump in and try and resolve these issues immediately which will often cause the client to react even further. During these times, the lawyer should allow the client to offload and get their frustrations out first before discussing the way forward. Taking the time to listen, making notes of the client's fears and problems will let the client know that the lawyer is there to do the very best you can for them. Following the conversation, ensure the lawyer have a realistic plan with achievable timelines and the client should know when they can expect to hear from the lawyer next. The lawyer should always follow this up with a written confirmation by email, post or via the firm's customer portal.

Following these steps is not a guaranteed way to client happiness and it will not be possible to please every client every time. Identifying issues early on will prevent the client experiencing "surprises" that risk clouding the trust and confidence the lawyer has taken time to build up. Being attentive and nurturing the client relationship ensures that clients are easier to work with. Learning to manage the client in a professional and appropriate manner enables the lawyer to not only meet their expectations, but often exceed them.

The internal client requires the same reassurances. Fellow professionals will be facing the same pressures and deadlines.

5.5 Acting ethically

Members of CILEX must adhere to the **CILEX Code of Conduct**. The Code is a set of principles that enable chartered legal executives to deliver prescribed outcomes relating to their conduct, practice and professional performance. The **Code of Conduct** is in place to ensure all members behave in an ethical manner that is open and honest. Acting ethically is at the centre of the client-lawyer relationship. The Code provides direction and guidance to deal with situations that may arise during the course of the case.

The Core Principles of the **CILEX Code of Conduct** are as follows:

> "You must:
>
> (1) Uphold the rule of law and the impartial administration of justice.
>
> (2) Maintain high standards of professional and personal conduct and justify public trust in you, your profession and the provision of legal services.
>
> (3) Behave with honesty and integrity.
>
> (4) Comply with your legal and regulatory obligations and deal with your regulators and ombudsmen openly, promptly and co-operatively.
>
> (5) Act competently in the best interests of your client and respect client confidentiality.
>
> (6) Treat everyone fairly and without prejudice.
>
> (7) Ensure your independence is not compromised.
>
> (8) Act effectively and in accordance with proper governance and sound financial and risk management principles.
>
> (9) Protect client money and assets."

If a law firm is regulated by the Solicitors Regulation Authority, all members of staff (not just solicitors) are required to comply with the **SRA Standards and Regulations** which set out similar detailed ethical requirements.

Note, in particular, the following Principles (see https://www.sra.org.uk/solicitors/standards-regulations/principles/):

"You act:

(1) in a way that upholds the constitutional principle of the rule of law, and the proper administration of justice.

(2) in a way that upholds public trust and confidence in the solicitors' profession and in legal services provided by authorised persons.

(3) with independence.

(4) with honesty.

(5) with integrity.

(6) in a way that encourages equality, diversity and inclusion.

(7) in the best interests of each client."

Knowledge checks!

(1) Which of the following is an internal client?

(a) Jones Building (Wrexham) Ltd whose managing director wants you to do the conveyancing for a purchase of new business premises

(b) Huw Rees-James, a local councillor in your district council

(c) The trade union Unison whose representative wants you to represent one of their members at an Employment Tribunal

(2) Match the following Core Principles in the CILEX Code of Conduct with the equivalent Principles in the **SRA Standards and Regulations**:

CILEX Core Principle	SRA Principle
1	6
5	1
6	7

5.6 Summary!

(1) External clients are relationships with individuals and organisations outside of the business. They include private clients, business clients, banks and building societies and trade unions. In addition, experts, such as medical experts, and providers of outsourced services are also in the category of external clients.

(2) Internal clients are relationships within the lawyer's own organisation. They include managers and councillors in local government and managers of other teams in large companies with in-house lawyers.

(3) Managing expectations is an important part of nurturing both external and internal clients. Regular communication is also crucial.

(4) Lawyers must comply with the relevant professional regulations and codes of conduct: the **CILEX Code of Conduct** and the **SRA Standards and Regulations**.

CHAPTER 6

Types of Business Structure

Aims of chapter!

This chapter will enable you to:

- Identify and explain the main features of sole traders, ordinary and limited liability partnerships and private companies limited by shares
- Identify some of the main issues which are likely to influence a client in their choice of business medium, and
- Explain the advantages and disadvantages of the types of business medium described in this chapter.

6.1 Introduction

This module introduces you to business law. Here, the main focus is going to be on partnerships and companies. But you shouldn't forget that a lot of businesses are run by individuals working alone. The law calls them sole traders. Some businesses are started by sole traders, who then progress to another form – sole traders may take on partners, or they may form a company – or they may even become a partnership first and then a company after that. A lot of businesses, though, are run by sole traders throughout their lifetime.

In this module you are going to look at the types of business structure, and the main differences between them. You are also going to look at the legislation which determines how they are set up and run. We shall be considering the following structures:

- sole traders;
- partnerships: general partnerships, limited partnerships and limited liability partnerships;
- companies: private companies limited by shares, public companies and companies limited by guarantee.

It can help to think of a hypothetical business and consider how the topics we are discussing relate to this. The box below sketches out such a business; we'll return to it later in this textbook.

Law in context!

Starting a new business

Samantha Jowett is 29 years old. After leaving school at the age of 18, she was employed for seven years as a cabinet maker. By 2016, the quality of her work was receiving much critical attention, with enthusiastic articles in magazines and trade journals. By then, she had become impatient with the attitudes of her employers. She felt they were too conservative, reluctant to embrace new designs or explore new lines of business, and unwilling to reward her appropriately for the commercial success she was bringing to their business.

Notwithstanding the unfavourable economic climate, Samantha decided the time was right to set up in business on her own. She took a lease of workshop premises in her native Manchester and rapidly built up a loyal clientele seeking expensive and individually designed pieces of furniture. She found that footballers, and their wives and girlfriends, were especially willing to pay the outrageously high prices her furniture commanded. Her range of bespoke cabinets for displaying sports trophies also proved very popular. Her main customers for these were football clubs, and her location in the north of England was an obvious advantage, being close to those teams capable of actually winning some silverware!

Initially, Samantha owned and ran the business alone, as a sole trader. In 2018 she took on her friend Maja Kowalska as a part time designer. She pays Maja a salary of £20,000 per year.

Samantha's business is now generating sales of around £120,000 each year. Her expenses, including rent, light, heat, the cost of materials and Maja's salary, are about £80,000 each year, so that her annual profit is around £40,000.

The business has now expanded considerably, and she needs additional capital to continue its growth. Maja has substantial savings, and she says that she is willing to invest up to £50,000 in the business, provided that "the terms are right". Samantha must now decide what legal form to use for her expanded business, given Maja's involvement. The main choices are between running the business as a partnership with Maja, and running it through a company.

Terminology!

Many people who are employed by a business will refer to their employer as "my company".

In many cases this will be incorrect. If the organisation is a sole trader (owned by only one person) or a partnership (with two or more partners) the correct description is "my firm". Only organisations which have complied with the formalities under the **Companies Act 2006** can correctly be described as companies.

6.2 Sole traders

Samantha is choosing between a partnership and a company, but at the moment she is running her business as a sole trader. Sole traders are everywhere. Take a look around you next time you are out and about. Look at small shops, or businesses like hairdressers or beauty parlours, or offices run by accountants, or insurance brokers – even lawyers. If the business is owned by a single individual, without any partners, and its name does not include "Limited", "Ltd" or "LLP", then it's almost certainly run by a sole trader.

6.2.1 What does it mean to be a sole trader?

Essentially, it means that Samantha **is** the business. Think of all the things that are used to run the business. They might include tools, machinery and furniture, and a phone.

These days, even a business like Samantha's is unlikely to manage without a computer, at least to create and manage correspondence and other documents, and quite possibly to use specialist design software. There will be stocks of materials, and also work in progress – projects that Samantha is working on, but which she hasn't yet completed or delivered to customers. All of these are the business's **assets**. Even though they are used in the business, they belong to Samantha personally.

The same thing applies to any **liabilities** relating to the business. Samantha is quite likely to be buying materials on credit – perhaps she will only pay for them at the end of each month. Until she pays for the materials, the money that she owes for them is a debt – a liability. She will have other debts too: rent, electricity and water bills, phone bills, internet charges and so on. Most businesses also need to borrow money, often from a bank. The simplest borrowing arrangement is an over- draft, to fund the business from day to day, until money comes in from customers. Again, all these debts relate to the business but they are owed by Samantha personally. If the debt is not paid, the person to whom the money is owed – we call them **creditors** – can sue Samantha for it. A creditor trying to enforce a debt against Samantha may be able to seize her personal assets – her bank account, her car and most importantly her house. If she cannot pay, they can have her declared bankrupt.

Personal liability is likely to be an even bigger worry for a business which risks being found liable to its customers or the public for breach of contract, or in tort. Think of an architect's practice, for example: if something goes wrong with an architect's design for a building, the whole project could be at risk, and there is also the possibility of liability to the public if the building turns out to be dangerous.

6.2.2 Business and personal affairs

At this point you might just be wondering whether Samantha actually has to separate out all the things that she uses for the business from the things that she uses in her personal life. Can she use the same phone for both? The same computer? Can she have an office in her home? The answer to this is that a sole trader does not have to separate their business assets – the things they own for use in the business – from their personal assets. Nor do they have to separate their business liabilities from their personal liabilities – so, for example, Samantha could use her personal bank overdraft to fund her business. A lot of sole traders running small businesses do just that.

However, Samantha is going to have to report her business income and business expenditure every year to HM Revenue & Customs (**HMRC**), and larger businesses also have to submit a balance sheet, which shows what the business owns and what it owes. HMRC have rules about exactly what counts as business income, and particularly what counts as business expenditure. In practice, Samantha is going to have to keep some form of **accounting records** for her business, so that she can provide the necessary information to HMRC. She will also want to keep accounts to allow her to track how well her business is performing, what it owns and what it owes. For all these reasons, sole traders normally need to maintain some degree of separation between their business and personal assets and liabilities, both so that they can meet HMRC's requirements and also so that they can monitor the business's performance.

6.2.3 Sole traders as employers

Sole traders do not necessarily have to work alone. If you think of a small shop – say a newsagent – it is quite likely that the owner will have help, from shop assistants, or teenagers delivering newspapers. In exactly the same way, Samantha employs Maja to help. Maja is an **employee**: Samantha employs her to work in the business. As we will see, all employees have an **employment contract** with their employer (you can have an employment contract even if nothing has been put in writing or signed). Maja, the employee, is one party to the employment contract. The other party is Samantha, Maja's employer. Running a business with employees does not stop you from being a sole trader. You are still in ultimate charge – you can tell your employees what to do. Also, if the business makes a profit, then that profit is yours – most employees are paid a salary, which is usually fixed.

6.2.4 Contracts

Sole traders enter into contracts relating to the business in their own name. If Samantha's business buys wood, it is Samantha who enters into the contract. If the wood is not delivered, it is Samantha who can sue the seller. If it is not paid for, the seller can sue Samantha for the money. If a sole trader shopkeeper employs a shop assistant, and the shop assistant sells something to a customer, there will be a contract with the customer. The shop assistant enters into that contract with the customer on behalf of the shopkeeper, so the other party to the contract is the shopkeeper (and not the assistant).

6.2.5 Legislation

What is the legislation governing how sole traders set up and run their businesses? Well actually there is not anything specific to sole traders. That is because they own the business alone, so there is no need for rules governing the relationship between the business owners. They run it on their own too, so there's no need for rules about management.

Of course, there is a lot of legislation out there which applies to all businesses, including sole traders. This legislation covers important areas such as employment law, taxation and business names.

6.2.6 Sole traders: advantages and disadvantages

Last of all, we should pause to consider the advantages and disadvantages of running a business as a sole trader. This will help when you start to think about the choice of business structure. Think for a moment about what might be the obvious pros and cons.

Sole trader: pros and cons	
Pro	**Con**
Simplicity	Personally liable for business's debts
Easy to set up	Cannot involve anyone closely in running the business without becoming a partnership
Lack of regulation	
Freedom to act independently	

Table 6.2

6.3 Partnerships

Samantha wants to involve Maja in her business. She is choosing between running her business as a partnership with Maja and running it as a company. We are going to look at these two options in turn.

6.3.1 What is a partnership?

Most "partnerships" are really no more than an arrangement between people who are running a business together. Suppose Samantha chooses to operate her business as a partnership with Maja. The law will see the partnership as a relationship between Samantha and Maja. The partnership is not a separate legal entity. It cannot own anything, or enter into contracts, or incur debts. Although we may talk loosely about "the partnership" owning land, selling cabinets, employing staff, borrowing money and the like, as far as the law is concerned it is the partners themselves who are doing all these things. Crucially, the partners themselves will be personally liable for, say, a breach of any contract, or for debts incurred by the partnership, in very much the same way as a sole trader.

Clearly, this makes the position of a partner just as risky as that of a sole trader – in fact even more so, because Samantha is also going to be liable for anything that Maja does as her partner. As we shall see later in this chapter, Samantha's position would be very different if she chose to run her business through a company rather than as a partnership.

6.3.2 Types of partnership

There are a number of different types of partnership. The most common is the **ordinary** or **general partnership**, governed by the **Partnership Act 1890** (**PA 1890**).

6.3.3 Limited liability partnerships: Limited Liability Partnerships Act 2000

Since 2001, another type of limited partnership can be created: the **limited liability partnership** (LLP). This business structure was established by the **Limited Liability Partnerships Act 2000**. LLPs exist as separate legal persons, in the same way as companies. This means that they can, for example, own property, enter into contracts and owe money. Their partners all enjoy limited liability. However, LLPs are run (and their partners are taxed) in very much the same way as ordinary partnerships.

They are becoming much more widely used. you can recognise an LLP because its name usually has "LLP" at the end (or, much less commonly, "Limited Liability Partnership"). Many LLPs are professional partnerships, owned and run by lawyers or accountants, for example. Next time you see a law firm's name, check to see whether it has "LLP" at the end. We are going to look at their main features in more detail later in this chapter.

6.4 Ordinary (or "general") partnerships

6.4.1 The law applicable to ordinary partnerships

Ordinary partnerships are governed by the **Partnership Act 1890** (**PA 1890**).

PA 1890 lays down a series of default rules, which will apply to ordinary partnerships unless the partners agree otherwise. Because the Act is based on pre-1890 case law, the rules that it contains can often seem out of date, and they may not be suitable for a modern partnership. A good example is the rules on the retirement of a partner: under **PA 1890,** the only way for a partner to leave a partnership is to dissolve it.

Fortunately, almost all of the rules in the Act can be overridden by an express agreement between the partners. Whilst many partnerships are formed without an express agreement, a legal adviser should always recommend that the partners draw up a full partnership agreement, to exclude the provisions in the Act and provide for areas of potential difficulty.

Just like sole traders, ordinary partnerships are subject to the rules in the **Companies Act 2006** on choice of business name.

6.4.2 What is an ordinary partnership?

NB All section numbers in this part of this chapter refer to **PA 1890** unless otherwise stated.

Essentially, an ordinary partnership exists when two or more people run a business together. Partnership is defined by **s1(1)** as:

> *the relation which subsists between persons carrying on a business in common with a view of profit.*

The definition is extremely important because, if it is fulfilled, a partnership will exist in law, whatever the people involved may have intended. This can have serious consequences. For example, each partner will be liable for the partnership's debts, to the full extent of their private assets.

The definition tells us whether a partnership exists. It can also be used to determine whether an individual is a partner: if they are carrying on business in common with other people with a view of profit then they will be a partner.

The definition identifies three characteristics which must be present before a partnership exists. There must be:

- a business in common;
- carried on for profit;
- by or on behalf of the partners.

6.4.3 A business in common

"Business" is defined in **s45** as including *every trade, occupation, or profession*. This statutory definition is rather imprecise. Not every occupation is a "business" for the purposes of partnership law. For example, a landowner who simply manages their land and collects rent from their tenants is not carrying on a business, but if they regularly bought and sold land this would constitute a business. For a business to exist, the enterprise must be one which has been recognised as a commercial trade or a profession – for example, plumbers or solicitors.

The idea of the business being carried on *in common* also raises difficulties. Merely owning something together does not create a partnership, unless the participants go further and carry on a business with a view to profit. Two people who jointly own a piece of land are not partners, even though they develop the land and later use it for their mutual benefit, unless they go further and use it to carry on a business. This point is confirmed by **s2(1)**, which provides:

> *Joint tenancy, tenancy in common, joint property, common property or part ownership does not of itself create a partnership as to anything so held or owned ...*

A "business" requires some continuing activity. It generally involves a series of acts which, if successful, result in a gain for the participants. A single deal may be a business within **PA 1890**, but only if it is complex enough.

In ***Khan and Another v Miah and Another [2000]*** it was held that a partnership may exist before trading is actually commenced. This case concerned a new restaurant. The partners had to acquire premises, secure planning consent and fit out the premises ready to carry on the restaurant business. The court held that committing money and effort to the process of preparing for business was part and parcel of being in partnership. Even before they started to trade, the partners were already involved in commercial activity with a view to profit.

Finally, you should note that certain professions prohibit their members from practising in partnership – a barrister, for example, cannot practise in partnership with another barrister. (Barristers often work closely together in "chambers" and share responsibility for employing clerks and other expenses, but they take great care not to share profits.)

6.4.4 Carried on with a view of profit

The business must be conducted with a profit motive. What about a partnership set up in order to save tax? In ***Newstead v Frost [1980]***, David Frost, a TV personality, formed a partnership for tax purposes. The UK tax authorities claimed that it was not carried on with a view of profit, since its purpose was to avoid tax. However, the House of Lords concluded that it was formed with a view to creating profits from David

Frost's various interests. That purpose was not overridden by the desire to avoid tax, although that was a major motive for structuring his interests in that particular way.

6.4.5 Determining whether there is a partnership

Sharing profits is one of the key characteristics that distinguishes a partnership from other relationships (e.g. employer and employee, or lender and borrower). **s2(3)** provides that receiving a share of profits raises a *presumption* that a person is a partner. But you need to be careful here: **s2(2)** says that sharing profits is not enough by itself to make someone a partner. The test under **s1(1)** is whether the partners are carrying on a *business in common* (with a view of profit). There are many other indicators which can also help to determine whether this test is met. other factors which would point to someone being a partner include whether they have:

- a financial interest in the business (for example, by investing capital);
- the right to be involved in decisions affecting the business;
- the right to examine the business's accounts;
- the right to insist on openness and honesty from their fellow partners;
- the right to block the introduction of a new partner; and
- the responsibility of sharing in any losses.

Ultimately, the answer is going to depend on the facts of the particular case. The courts will look at anything that has been expressly agreed between the parties. The way in which the business is run in practice may also be evidence of a tacit agreement. For example, regularly taking part in management decisions may make someone a partner, even if there is a written agreement between the parties which makes no mention of it.

In most cases, it is not difficult to tell whether there is a partnership, or who is a partner. But problems can arise, for example with so-called "salaried partners". Salaried partners are found in many professional firms – for example, lawyers' and accountancy practices. They have the title of "partner", but they are paid a salary rather than sharing in profits. If they are really partners, this means that they will share liability for the firm's debts, and unless there is an agreement to the contrary, they will have the other rights which are granted to partners by the default provisions in **PA 1890**. Whether a salaried partner is really a partner will depend whether they are "carrying on business with a view of profit", and a court will look at all the factors to decide whether the test is met.

6.4.6 Factors which are not sufficient to constitute a partnership

After saying that sharing in profits raises a presumption that a person is a partner, **s2(3)** goes on to list a series of factors which by themselves are **not** sufficient to make someone a partner. These include:

- receiving payment of a debt or "liquidated" (fixed) amount – even if that amount is payable only if there are profits available;
- paying an employee wages calculated as a share of a business's profits;
- paying the widow, widower or child of a deceased partner a pension calculated as a share of the business's profits.

6.4.7 Ordinary partnerships: advantages and disadvantages

The main advantage of an ordinary partnership is its simplicity. In theory, to form a partnership it is sufficient to fulfil the definition in **s1(1)**. In practice, however, a legal adviser should always recommend preparing a proper partnership agreement.

Some other considerations are:

Ordinary partnership: pros and cons	
Pro	**Con**
Easy to form – but in practice should always prepare partnership agreement	Personally liable for debts of whole business
Less regulation than LLPs and companies	Ceases to exist if all but one partners leave or die
No need to prepare and publish detailed accounts – cheaper and more private	
Partnership agreement private and can be kept confidential	
Management: unless otherwise agreed, each partner has equal rights	

Table 6.4

6.5 Limited liability partnerships

6.5.1 What is an LLP?

Whilst an LLP is called a "partnership", unlike an ordinary partnership an LLP exists as a **separate legal person**. If Samantha formed an LLP to run her business with Maja, the LLP (rather than Samantha and Maja personally) would own the business's assets, enter into contracts, employ people, sell its finished products and so on. It could also borrow money, and it would be liable under all those various contracts if things went wrong. Neither Samantha nor Maja would be liable. In that sense, the liability of partners in an LLP is "limited".

Because it exists as a separate legal person, forming an LLP requires more formalities than an ordinary partnership. The process of forming LLPs (and also companies) is managed by a government authority called the **Registrar of Companies**, based at Companies House in Cardiff. An LLP is formed by completing specified documents and filing them with the Registrar.

6.5.2 Disclosure obligations

The principle of limited liability can work to the disadvantage of an LLP's creditors – the people to whom it owes money. If an LLP becomes insolvent or is wound up, the creditors may not be able to claim against the LLP's partners. To protect creditors, LLPs are subject to disclosure obligations. In particular, they must prepare financial accounts and publish them in the same way as a company. Depending on their size, LLPs may also need to have their accounts audited.

They must also file certain other information with the Registrar of Companies, who will place it on a publicly accessible register so as to prevent their partners from using the LLP as a front to conceal their identity. For example, the Registrar keeps a record of the names of the partners in the LLP, and any changes must be notified to them.

6.5.3 Continues in existence

Because the LLP is a legal person separate from its partners, it will continue in existence until it is dissolved, even if all its partners retire or die.

6.5.4 Default statutory rules

However, in many other ways an LLP is similar to an ordinary partnership. There is a set of default statutory rules which will apply to relations between the individual partners, and the partners and the LLP, unless the partners agree otherwise. In fact, these rules are surprisingly similar to the default rules in **PA 1890**. So, for example, the default rule is that every partner has an equal right to manage the business.

In practice, just as with an ordinary partnership, you should advise an LLP's partners to enter into a detailed agreement (called an "LLP agreement") which will override the default rules and deal with areas of potential difficulty. This LLP agreement is a private document: it is not filed with the Registrar of Companies.

6.5.5 The law applicable to LLPs

The principal statute governing LLPs is the **Limited Liability Partnerships Act 2000**. This Act is supplemented by the **Limited Liability Partnerships Regulations 2001**. These Regulations contain the default rules which apply between partners unless they are overridden by agreement.

LLPs are also subject to various other pieces of legislation which normally apply to companies. For example, the rules on preparing and auditing accounts, which are similar to the rules applicable to companies, are contained in the **Companies Act 2006**. LLPs and their partners are also subject to various rules in the **Insolvency Act 1986** which normally apply to company directors. The rules on business names in the **Companies Act 2006** which apply to sole traders and ordinary partnerships are also applicable to LLPs.

6.5.6 LLPs: advantages and disadvantages

Samantha could choose to take Maja into business as a partner in a new LLP. Actually, this would be unusual: LLPs tend to be used by professional firms seeking the benefit of limited liability. It is less usual – though not unheard of – for a trading or manufacturing business such as Samantha's to be run as an LLP. Advantages and disadvantages include:

LLP: pros and cons	
Pro	**Con**
Limited liability	Formation: requires registration
Less regulation than a limited company	More regulation than an ordinary partnership
Management: unless otherwise agreed, each partner has equal rights	Need to prepare and file accounts, which in many cases must also be audited
LLP agreement private and can be kept confidential	Publicity: financial information and certain information relating to partnership and partners
Perpetual succession: continues in existence until dissolved	

Table 6.5

6.6 Companies

The final option open to Samantha is to form a company with Maja. The key defining feature of a company is that, like an LLP, it exists as a separate legal person. That means that, like an LLP, it can own property, enter into contracts and incur liabilities. A creditor who wants to enforce a liability incurred by the company must bring their claim against the company.

If Samantha and Maja formed a company, they would own shares in it. The owners of a company are called its **members**, or **shareholders**. Companies are managed by their **directors**. This separation of ownership and management is another important feature of companies. However, in small companies like this one the shareholders and directors are often the same people.

The process of forming a company is call **incorporation**. Like an LLP, a company is formed by completing specified documents and filing them for publication with the Registrar of Companies at Companies House.

The process of administering and running a company is generally more complicated than for partnerships or LLPs. One reason is the separation of ownership and management: rules are needed to specify which decisions are taken by the members and which are taken by the directors. other rules are needed to protect the members from improper conduct by the directors. All companies have an internal constitution, called the **articles of association**, where some of these rules are set out.

Again, similar to an LLP, companies must file information with Companies House, where it is placed on a public register. The filing requirements are, however, more complex than for an LLP – for example, certain types of decisions by the members need to be recorded at Companies House. The articles of association (unlike a partnership agreement or an LLP agreement) are also a public document.

6.6.1 Separate legal personality

The principle that companies have separate legal personality in English law was confirmed in the leading House of Lords decision in ***Salomon v A Salomon & Co Ltd [1897]***. This case explored the legal relationship between the company and its major shareholder, Aaron Salomon, who was also its managing director. He had also lent money to the company, making him its major creditor.

The decision confirmed the following principles:

- A company is a legal entity, distinct and separate from its members. Therefore, even if all the shares in a company are owned by just one person, that person will not be treated as the company, or as responsible for the company's debts. This principle of separation also means that a member (even a member who controls the company) can lend money to the company and take security from the company for the loan (as Aaron Salomon himself did) or be employed by the company.

- A company's assets are its own. They do not belong to the company's members. Hence, for example, a policy insuring the company's property – say its land, or its vehicles, or stocks of goods that it intends to sell – against fire or theft must be taken out in the company's name, and not in the name of a member. The members' interest in the company's assets is indirect, through the shares that they own.
- The liability of the members for the company's debts is usually limited to the amount that they have agreed to pay for their shares. In other words, the members can be required to pay the full price of their shares to the company (if they have not already done so), but beyond that generally they will have no further liability.
- A company may exist in perpetuity. Its existence will not be affected by changes in the composition and identity of the members and the directors. A company can cease to exist only through a process known as dissolution.

6.6.2 Types of company

6.6.2.1 Companies limited by shares

The overwhelming majority of companies are **companies limited by shares**. That means that the company's members own shares in the company, as Samantha and Maja would do in our example. It is for this reason that the members of a company limited by shares are known as its shareholders.

6.6.2.2 Other types of company

There are other types of company, although they are found much less frequently.

One of these is the **company limited by guarantee**. Companies limited by guarantee are owned by their members, but the members do not own shares in the company (and so they are not "shareholders"). The members guarantee to contribute a specified amount to the company's debts if required. Their liability is "limited" because they have no liability beyond the amount of their guarantee.

Useful link!

Companies limited by guarantee are most often charitable or not-for-profit organisations. **NB** The CILEX Foundation, which provides scholarships and bursaries to students (https://www.cilex.org.uk/membership/cilex_foundation/) is a company limited by guarantee.

Another type of company is the **unlimited company**. An unlimited company is similar to a company limited by shares, with the difference that the liability of its shareholders is not limited.

The **Community Interest Group** (**CIG**) is also a type of company. CIGs are formed under the **Companies (Audit, Investigations and Community Enterprise) Act 2004**. They are intended for use particularly by businesses with social, community or environmental objectives, but which do not qualify as charities. They differ from companies limited by shares mainly in that they are formed for a particular purpose.

We shall not be considering CIGs, companies limited by guarantee or unlimited companies further in this course book.

6.6.2.3 Companies limited by shares: public and private

Companies limited by shares can be either public or private. Both sorts can easily be recognised by their name. A **private company limited by**

shares has to have "Limited", or "Ltd" (or the Welsh "Cyfyngedig" or "Cyf") at the end of its name. A public company limited by shares is known as a **public limited company** (or **PLC**). They must have "Public Limited Company", or "PLC" (or the Welsh equivalent) at the end of their name. You can see these abbreviations everywhere – look out for them in advertisements, on signboards, name plates, websites and so on.

The crucial difference between a private company limited by shares and a PLC is that a private limited company is prohibited from offering its shares to the public. PLCs can raise capital by offering their shares to the public, and in fact the shares of many (but by no means all) PLCs are traded on public stock markets. Because PLCs can offer their shares to the public, they are subject to a much higher standard of regulation, in order to protect those who invest in them.

If they chose to form a company, Samantha and Maja would almost certainly use a private company limited by shares. That is the type of company on which we are going to concentrate in this course book.

6.6.3 The law applicable to companies

Companies are a creation of statute law. There has been a series of Companies Acts, going back into the 19th century. The current Act is the **Companies Act 2006** (**CA 2006**) (which replaced the **Companies Act 1985**). **CA 2006** is a substantial statute, with no less than 1,300 sections.

Besides **CA 2006**, companies are subject to a wide range of further legislation. This includes:

- The **Companies (Model Articles) Regulations 2008**. A company's members are largely free to choose its articles of association. The Model Articles Regulations provide sets of default **Model Articles** for both private companies limited by shares and PLCs. A newly-created company will automatically adopt these Model Articles unless the people forming the company decide otherwise.

- The **Company Directors Disqualification Act 1986** (**CDDA 1986**). Company directors are subject to wide-ranging regulation, both in **CA 2006** and elsewhere. **CDDA 1986** allows courts to impose a period of disqualification on a director who has fallen below the required standard, particularly where the director's company has become insolvent.
- The **Insolvency Act 1986** (**IA 1986**). Amongst other things, **IA 1986** sets out the rules under which a company can be dissolved (which it refers to as **winding up**). This can happen when a company becomes insolvent. **IA 1986** also deals with winding up solvent companies.
- The **Economic Crime and Corporate Transparency Act 2023** has introduced identity verification for new and existing company directors, people with significant control (PSCs) and those delivering documents to the companies register. The Act has also tightened controls over limited liability partnerships and strengthened information sharing and enforcement powers in relation to anti-money laundering.

6.6.4 Companies: advantages and disadvantages

Samantha and Maja could form a private company limited by shares. Advantages would include limited liability, and separation of ownership and management – this can be an advantage where a business is seeking investors who do not want to be involved in day-to-day management. Advantages and disadvantages include:

Private company: pros and cons	
Pro	**Con**
Limited liability	Formation: requires registration
Separation of ownership and management	Separation of ownership and management makes administration more complex

Private company: pros and cons	
Pro	**Con**
Can raise finance by offering shares to investors who do not want to become involved in management	Need to prepare and file accounts, which in many cases must also be audited
Perpetual succession: continues in existence until dissolved	Publicity: financial information, certain information relating to members and directors, constitution and some decisions

Table 6.6

The tax regime for companies is also different from that of partnerships and LLPs. The tax treatment is often one of the most important considerations in the choice of legal forms.

Knowledge checks!

(1) Complete the gap in the definition of a partnership in **s1(1) Partnership Act 1990**:

the relation which subsists between persons carrying on a business in common with a view of ....

(a) Profitability

(b) Income

(c) Profit

(d) Solvency

(2) The members of a company are responsible for its management. True or false?

(a) False

(b) True

6.7 Summary!

(1) A **sole trader** is an individual carrying on a business. There is no legal separation between the assets and liabilities of the business and those of the individual sole trader. A sole trader's liability is therefore unlimited.

(2) A **partnership** – an ordinary partnership – is defined as a relationship. It is the relationship which subsists between persons who carry on business in common with a view of profit. A partnership does not have separate legal personality, so in reality the partnership's assets and liabilities are the assets and liabilities of the individual partners.

(3) There will be a partnership if the definition is satisfied, and everyone falling within the definition will be a partner.

(4) Partnerships are governed by **PA 1890**, which implies default rules which will apply between the partners if nothing else is agreed. In practice, partners should be advised to agree their own rules in a partnership agreement, which will override the default rules.

(5) Like sole traders, partners in a partnership have unlimited liability for its obligations.

(6) A **limited liability partnership** differs from an ordinary partnership in that it exists as a separate legal person.

(7) As with an ordinary partnership, an LLP is governed by default rules which apply unless they have been varied by express agreement. The partners should be advised to agree their own rules in an LLP agreement.

(8) Partners in an LLP benefit from limited liability.

(9) Like an LLP, a **private company limited by shares** exists as a separate legal person.

(10) A company is owned by its members and managed by its directors.

(11) A company's internal constitution is contained in its articles of association. The articles are a public document.

(12) The liability of the members of a private company limited by shares is limited to the amount that they have agreed to pay for their shares.

CHAPTER 7

Starting a Business as a Company

Aims of chapter!

This chapter will enable you to:

- Explain the matters to be considered when setting up a private company limited by shares
- Describe the procedure to be followed when setting up such a company
- Explain the role and responsibilities of a company's promoters, and how to deal with pre-incorporation contracts, and
- Advise on the matters which need to be considered once a company has been formed.

7.1 Introduction

In **Chapter 6** you read that a company is a separate legal person, owned by its **members** and managed by its **directors**. In most companies, the members own **shares** in the company and are called **shareholders**. Also, most companies are **limited companies**, meaning that the liability of their members is limited. In the case of a **company limited by shares**, the shareholders' liability is limited to the amount that they have agreed to pay for their shares.

In this chapter you will read how to form a **private company limited by shares** (referred to in this course book as a **private company**), which is the type of company which is most frequently encountered in the United Kingdom.

The other common form of company is the **public limited company** (**PLC**). The essential difference between a private company and a PLC is that a private company is prohibited from offering its shares to the public. Because this prohibition does not apply to PLCs, they are subject to much more regulation, in order to protect the public who invest in them.

In this chapter you will read mainly about the matters to be considered when setting up a private company, and the procedure that must be followed. you will also look at the position of a company's **promoters** – the people who form the company. Finally, you will read about the matters which the company's directors need to consider once the company has been formed.

Unless otherwise stated, references in this chapter to section numbers are to sections of the **Companies Act 2006** (**CA 2006**).

In this chapter we are going to use the example of Samantha Jowett, whom you first encountered in **Chapter 6**.

Law in context!

Converting a business to a limited company

Samantha Jowett runs a business in Manchester designing and manufacturing bespoke furniture, including cabinets for displaying sports trophies. She runs the business as a sole trader, and employs her friend Maja Kowalska as a part time designer.

The business needs additional capital in order to continue its growth. Maja is prepared to invest up to £50,000. Samantha has now decided that she will convert it into a private company. Samantha and Maja will be the company's shareholders and directors. Samantha will contribute the assets of the existing business, which she has had valued at £200,000, and Maja will contribute £50,000 in cash.

7.2 Matters to be considered

The process of forming a company is similar to the procedure that you read about in **Chapter 5** in relation to LLPs. A form is sent to the Registrar of Companies at Companies House and a fee is paid. However, either one or two further documents are required for a company: a **memorandum of association** is required in any case, and **articles of association** may also be needed. If everything is in order, the Registrar then issues a **certificate of incorporation**.

The additional complexities involved in forming a company compared to an LLP make it essential to consider a number of matters before any steps are taken. These should be discussed with the client.

7.2.1 Articles of association

A company's **articles of association** are the main part of its internal constitution. **s33** says that a company's constitution is binding on the company and its members in the same way as a contract between them.

The client needs to decide whether the company's articles will be the **Model Articles for Private Companies Limited by Shares** (the **Model Articles**, or **MA**), or whether instead the company will have its own **bespoke articles** (which may be a complete set of articles of association, or which may consist of the Model Articles with some specific amendments). If the company is to be formed with the Model Articles, there is no need to submit any articles of association with the application for registration – the Model Articles will then apply automatically. If the company is to have bespoke articles, they must be submitted with the application, and they will be available for public inspection at Companies House.

The Model Articles are contained in the **Companies (Model Articles) Regulations 2008**. When reading the Regulations, you need to take care to find the correct set of model articles. This is because the Regulations contain model articles for PLCs as well as private companies.

Individual articles in bespoke articles of association are often referred to as **special articles**.

A company can change its articles of association by set procedures.

7.2.2 "Shelf" company or "tailor-made" company?

A **shelf company** is a company that has already been formed and is kept ready to be sold to parties who want to use it. Shelf companies are normally formed and owned by specialised company formation agencies. Some large law firms may also form shelf companies and hold a stock of them ready for use by clients.

In contrast, a **tailor-made** company is one which is formed specifically for use by a particular client.

The main factor when considering whether to form a tailor-made company or to use a shelf company is speed. A tailor-made company's documentation can be drafted to suit the client's particular requirements and it will have a name chosen by the client. There will be a delay between taking instructions and incorporating the company.

A shelf company can be made available immediately, but work will be required to adapt it to the client's requirements. In particular:

- the shelf company's shareholders will have been nominated by the agency or law firm which formed it. (In practice, the initial shareholders of a shelf company are usually themselves companies.) It will be necessary to transfer the shares in the shelf company to the client before the shelf company can take any major decisions;
- the shelf company's directors will also have been appointed on its formation. They will need to appoint new directors, and the first directors will need to resign, before any steps can be taken to manage the shelf company. (Note that the new directors should be appointed before the first directors resign, to avoid a situation where there are no directors);
- the shelf company will have been formed with the absolute minimum number of shares and the absolute minimum amount of capital. one of the first steps that usually needs to be taken is to issue more shares. This will allow everyone who is intended to own a stake in the business to become shareholders. They may be required to make a substantial investment in return for their shares;
- the client may want the company to have bespoke articles, and in that case it will be necessary to change the articles of association. Drafting bespoke articles is the single most expensive task when forming a tailor-made company, and a client who wants bespoke articles cannot avoid it by purchasing a shelf company;

- shelf companies are usually formed with very artificial names, and the client is likely to want to change the name;
- the shelf company's registered office will be at the address of the agency or law firm which formed it. It will probably be necessary to change this.

7.2.3 Initial shareholders and directors

7.2.3.1 Initial shareholders

The persons who form a company and become its first shareholders are called its **subscribers**. **s7** says that a private company limited by shares can be formed by a single subscriber. In that case, if it is intended that there should be more than one shareholder it will be necessary to issue further shares to the other shareholders after the company has been formed. Suppose that in our example Samantha Jowett is the sole subscriber when her company is formed. In that case she will be the sole shareholder on formation. If Maja is to become a shareholder, it will be necessary to issue at least one share to her after the company has been created.

The subscriber or subscribers must be named in the incorporation document, and so the client must be asked who they will be. They can be individuals or companies. The client may also need to provide quite detailed information about their identity, for inclusion in the incorporation document.

7.2.3.2 Initial directors

s154(1) provides that a private company must also have at least one director, and so the client must be asked who the first director or directors will be. Directors are subject to some quite onerous obligations. Because of this, each director needs to consent to being appointed. It is possible to appoint further directors after the company has been formed. So in our example Samantha could be named as the sole first director. If Maja is also to be a director, Samantha could appoint her later.

In a small company, it is quite usual for the shareholders and directors to be the same people. This allows all the shareholders a direct say in the management of the company. Be aware that the rules applicable to shareholders and directors are very different. This makes it important, where the shareholders and directors are the same people, to be very clear when they are acting as shareholders and when they are acting as directors.

7.2.4 Initial share capital

A company's **share capital** is the amount of money payable to the company in return for its shares. A new company can be financed from its share capital, or by loans, or by a combination of both. There is no minimum amount of share capital required to form a private company, and in fact many private companies are formed with just £1 or £2 of share capital, or perhaps £100. For example, Samantha's company could be formed with just one £1 ordinary share. ("£1" refers to the capital payable on each share, sometimes called its **nominal value**. It is normal to call shares **ordinary shares**, to distinguish them from other special types of share such as preference shares.)

What is more, in a private company there is no absolute requirement that the share capital actually be **paid up** – in other words, it need not actually be paid to the company. If a share is not paid up, the amount payable on the share remains a debt payable by the shareholder to the company, and the shareholder can be required to pay it if the company becomes insolvent. However, the Model Articles require that all shares other than the shares taken by the subscribers when the company is formed must be fully paid up (see **MA21**). So, it will be necessary to adopt bespoke articles if it is intended that the company will issue shares which are not fully paid.

The client must therefore be asked what the initial share capital will be. If it is not going to be enough to finance the company, it will be necessary to raise further money, by issuing more shares after incorporation and/or by borrowing.

Samantha's company could be formed with her subscribing for just one £1 ordinary share, paid or unpaid. If that happened, once the company was formed Samantha would transfer the assets of her existing business to it in return for more shares, and Maja would also invest her £50,000 in return for shares. The assets of Samantha's business are valued at £200,000, and so she would probably be issued a further 199,999 shares, whilst Maja would receive 50,000 shares.

7.2.5 Company secretary

The company secretary takes responsibility for compliance with the administrative rules relating to the running of the company – issuing notices of meetings, taking minutes, filings at Companies House, keeping records and so on. There is no requirement for a private company to have a company secretary. If there is no company secretary, the administrative duties just mentioned are the responsibility of the directors. If a private company has a company secretary, they do not require any particular qualifications. They may also be a director of the company.

The directors and secretary (if any) are referred to together as the company's **officers**.

The client should therefore be asked whether the company will have a secretary. If so, it will be necessary to provide details of the secretary, and the secretary should consent to act in the same way as the director or directors. If no company secretary is appointed on formation, it is always possible to appoint one later.

7.2.6 Registered office

Like an LLP, a company must have a registered office, details of which must be provided when it is incorporated. The registered office is where the company's records will normally be kept, and where official correspondence, including documents commencing court proceedings, can be sent. Under **s86(2) CA 2006** a company must ensure that it has an "appropriate address" where in the ordinary course of events:

(a) a document addressed to the company, and delivered there by hand or by post, would be expected to come to the attention of a person acting on behalf of the company; and

(b) the delivery of documents there is capable of being recorded by the obtaining of an acknowledgement of delivery.

The law applicable to companies with a registered office in Scotland or Northern Ireland is different in some ways from that governing companies with a registered office in England or Wales. A client wishing to set up a company with its registered office in Scotland or Northern Ireland may need to take local legal advice.

7.2.7 Company name

s59 requires that (with a very few exceptions, including companies which are charities) a private company's name must end in "limited" or "ltd". If the company's registered office is situated in Wales, it can use one of the Welsh equivalents instead. These are "cyfyngedig" or "cyf".

Most of the other rules relating to company names are the same as the rules for the names of LLPs, which you read about in **Chapter 5**. Thus, a company cannot be registered with a name under which an existing LLP or company is already registered. You should search the Companies House index of names before choosing a name for a new company. You should also carry out a search of the trade marks register, and check trade directories and carry out an internet search, in order to minimise the risk of infringing a trade mark or a passing off action.

The rules on offensive names and names whose use would constitute an offence, and "sensitive" names and names suggesting a connection with the government, are the same as for LLPs, and are contained in **ss53–55**.

Like a sole trader, an ordinary partnership or an LLP, a company can choose a business name which is different from its own name – and indeed many companies do that. In that case, it will be subject to the usual rules on choice of business name.

7.3 The process of incorporation

s7 provides that a company is formed by one or more persons:

- subscribing their names to a **memorandum of association**; and
- complying with the requirements in **ss9–13**.

The memorandum of association must be filed at Companies House together with **Form IN01**, which contains all the other information required, and the fee. If the company is to have bespoke articles rather than the model articles then those must be filed too.

Note that (unlike a partnership or an LLP) a company does not need to be formed for the purpose of carrying on a business or generating a profit. This means that a company can be formed, for example, for charitable purposes. In practice, most charitable companies are limited by guarantee rather than by shares.

7.3.1 Memorandum of association

The **memorandum of association** is a simple document. It states that the subscribers agree to form a company, that they agree to become members and (in the case of a company with a share capital) that they agree to take at least one share each. Its form is specified in the **Companies (Registration) Regulations 2008**. The specified form requires each subscriber to state how many shares they are taking. A memorandum containing any additional material is likely to be rejected.

The memorandum has to be "authenticated", meaning that it must be signed by each subscriber or authenticated electronically in a manner acceptable to Companies House.

7.3.2 Form IN01

You can access Form IN01 using this link: https://www.gov.uk/government/publications/register-a-private-or-public-company-in01. You should have a copy of the paper form open in front of you as you read the explanation below (the £50 fee is not payable until the form is submitted for registration).

It must contain:

- the company's name;
- the type of company being formed;
- a statement of the company's principal business activity. If possible, this is to be provided by reference to a standard business classification code;
- details of the company's registered office;
- the company's choice of articles of association;
- the company's registered email address, which is not shown on the public record;
- details of the company secretary (if any) and the directors;
- a **statement of capital**, which sets out the amount of the company's share capital and the rights attaching to the shares. This will be straightforward where the company has only one class of ordinary shares. Companies can have more than one class of shares (for example, with different voting rights, or different rights to share in the company's profits). Prescribed particulars of the voting rights attached to the different classes of share must be set out;
- the initial shareholdings of each subscriber (at the time of incorporation);
- most of the remainder of the form is concerned with details of any **persons of significant control**. This is a complicated topic, and it is outlined below;

- confirmation by the subscribers that the director or directors and the company secretary (if any) have agreed to act;
- a **lawful purpose statement** confirming that the subscribers wish to form the company for lawful purposes;
- a **statement of compliance**. This needs to be signed by all the subscribers, or else someone acting on their behalf (referred to in Form IN01 as an "agent").

7.3.3 Persons of significant control (PSCs)

Essentially, a PSC is an individual who:

- owns or controls more than 25 per cent of the voting rights in a company (or LLP); or
- has the right to appoint or remove a majority of the board of directors; or
- has the right to exercise, or actually exercises, significant control over the company.

A shareholder in a company normally has one vote per share, and a shareholder holding more than 50 per cent of the shares normally has enough votes to appoint or remove a director. In the case of Samantha's company, assuming that she holds 200,000 shares and Maja holds 50,000, Samantha will own 80 per cent of the voting rights and so she will be a PSC. Maja will own only 20 per cent of the voting rights. This will not be enough to make her a PSC.

The second and third alternatives are designed to catch people who exercise substantial control over a company (or an LLP) other than by virtue of their voting rights. For example, the shareholders may agree in a contract that someone can appoint a majority of the directors, even though that person holds only very few shares – or even no shares at all. That person may not have enough votes to appoint the directors, but the agreement may require the shareholders to exercise their own votes in the way that the person directs. In that case, the person with the right to appoint the directors will be a PSC under the second alternative.

The third alternative catches someone who has neither 25 per cent of the votes, nor the right to appoint or remove a majority of the directors, but who has some other right to exercise significant control over the company – or who actually does so, even though they do not have a right to do so. Suppose, for example, that Samantha's wife Hilary is the brains behind her business, and that Samantha and Maja always do what she says. That would make Hilary a PSC. This is a rather unusual example but imagine instead the situation where a criminal "launders" their profits by passing them through a company. They have no shares in the company, and no right to appoint or remove directors, but they control the company because its shareholders and directors always do what they say. That would make them a PSC.

7.3.3.1 Relevant legal entities and other registrable persons

As well as PSCs, the rules cover **relevant legal entities** (**RLEs**). An RLE is an entity which is not an individual, but which otherwise meets the requirements for a PSC. So, for example, a company which owns 40 per cent of the shares in another company – and thus 40 per cent of the voting rights – would be an RLE.

7.3.4 Filing the incorporation documents

In the same way as for LLPs, the incorporation documents can be filed electronically or delivered in hard copy to Companies House by hand or by post. Electronic filing of company incorporation documents requires specialist software in the same way as it does when incorporating an LLP. For company formation, Companies House currently also offers a web incorporation service. This is not available where the company is being formed with bespoke articles – the company must be formed with Model Articles. The service is open 24 hours a day, 7 days a week, and is operated using a simple user log-in and password. If the application is accepted, a certificate of incorporation will be emailed to the applicant within two days.

7.3.5 Identity verification

The **Economic Crime and Corporate Transparency Act 2023** has amended **CA 2006** and introduced a requirement for company officers and persons of significant control to have their identity verified. This is intended to stop fraudulent appointments reaching the Companies House register as part of the government's efforts to combat money-laundering and other criminal activity.

There will be two types of identity verification.

(1) **Direct verification**

Individuals will be able to link their identity directly with Companies House using a photograph of their face and an identity document such as a passport or driving licence. other non-digital methods will be available.

(2) **Authorised corporate service providers**

Certain corporate service providers, such as accountants, legal advisers and company formation agents, will be able to deliver documents to the registrar. They must be registered with a supervisory body for anti-money laundering purposes (e.g. CILEX Regulation or the SRA). These corporate service providers will be able to carry out the identity verification checks.

Useful link!

Further details of the changes are set out at:

https://companieshouse.blog.gov.uk/2022/12/12/companies-house-reform-identity-verification/ .

7.4 The company's promoters

A company's **promoters** are the entrepreneurs who set it up. They may obtain investments in the company from outsiders, and they may sell assets to it – like Samantha, who is selling her business assets to her new company. Both of these possibilities allow scope for abuse, and rules have been developed to prevent this.

A further issue with promoters is that they may – quite properly – incur expenses in connection with the formation of the company – for example, legal advice, or incorporation fees. They may also enter into contracts and other arrangements in relation to the company before it has been formed. The difficulty here is that the promoters have to spend this money or conclude these contracts in their own name. They cannot say that they are acting as the company's agent because the company did not exist when the expense was incurred or the contract was entered into. Nonetheless, it may be appropriate for the company to reimburse the promoter's expenditure, or for the company, and not the promoter, to be bound by the contract once the company has been formed.

We therefore need to look at the rules which exist to prevent abuse by promoters, and also the rules on pre-incorporation contracts. Before we do that, we must consider exactly who is a promoter.

7.4.1 Who is a promoter?

Every company has at least one promoter. The term is not defined in **CA 2006**. The classic definition was given in ***Twycross v Grant [1877]***: *"one who undertakes to form a company with reference to a given project and to set it going, and who takes the necessary steps to accomplish that purpose"*. The definition is now understood to include anyone who:

- **either** takes the procedural steps necessary to form the company;
- **or** sets up the company's business (involving entering into pre-incorporation contracts);
- but **not those** who act merely in a professional capacity acting on the instructions of a promoter, for example, a lawyer or an accountant.

In registering her new company, Samantha is likely to be acting as a promoter. On the other hand, a law firm which acts on its formation will **not** be a promoter.

7.4.2 Preventing abuse by promoters

A good example of the potential for abuse by promoters is ***Erlanger v New Sombrero Phosphate Co [1878]***. Mr Erlanger acquired the lease of a phosphate mine in the West Indies for £55,000. He then formed a new company and sold his mining rights to it for £110,000. The purchase was approved by the company's directors, who had been appointed by Erlanger. Some of them were under his influence; others simply did not have enough time to look after the business. The document that offered the company's shares to the public did not disclose Mr Erlanger's profit. The original directors were then replaced. The new directors, on discovering the swindle, sued Erlanger for rescission (cancellation) of the contract for the sale of the mining rights. It was held that the contract should be rescinded because Erlanger had not properly disclosed his profit and therefore could not keep it.

This case illustrates how promoters of a company owe fiduciary duties. Crucially, a promoter must not make a secret profit. The promoter can avoid contravening this requirement by properly disclosing any profit they have made to either an independent board of directors or to the existing or prospective members of the company. This avoids any element of secrecy. If the promoter discloses any profit that they have made, they will be allowed to keep it. Otherwise, the company may elect to rescind the contract (as in ***Erlanger***). Where rescission is not available, the company can require the promoter to account for their profit.

Many of the cases on promoters' fiduciary duties date from the 19th century. The problems which gave rise to those cases arise much less frequently today. A major reason for this is the restrictions on companies offering shares to the public, only PLCs can do this now. PLCs are subject to much tighter regulation and disclosure requirements. A promoter of a private company could still, in theory, abuse their role by inviting selected investors to buy shares in the company.

7.4.3 Pre-incorporation contracts and expenditure

(1) **Pre-incorporation contracts**

As you have just seen, the problem with pre-incorporation contracts is that they are entered into at a time before the company exists. The law of agency does not allow an agent to act on behalf of a non-existent person, so promoters who enter into pre-incorporation contracts or incur pre-incorporation expenditure can do so only in their own name. The problem for promoters is how to ensure that the new company – when it is eventually formed – will become liable for obligations assumed before it was incorporated, and that the promoters will cease to be liable when it has been formed.

The answer to this question is now provided by **s51**. **s51** says that a contract which purports to be made by or on behalf of a company which has not been formed takes effect as one made with the person purporting to act on behalf of the company. In other words, the promoter is liable and not the company. However, this rule applies *subject to any agreement to the contrary*. In other words, promoters can avoid the problem by expressly agreeing with the other party to the contract that the contract is made with the company and not with the promoter.

(2) **Pre-incorporation expenditure**

Thus, by using careful wording a promoter can avoid liability under pre-incorporation contracts, and ensure that the company will be bound by them instead once it is formed. This will not necessarily help promoters with all pre-incorporation expenditure. There may not be an express contract with the party to whom the money is paid, and the money may have to be paid before the company is formed. To take a simple example, Companies House fees have to be paid when the incorporation documents are submitted. Can promoters recover this expenditure once the company has been formed?

The solution to this problem is for the new company to agree after it has been formed that it will approve any expenditure incurred in connection with its formation and reimburse the promoters for that expenditure.

7.5 Matters to be dealt with after formation

Once the company has been formed, there will be legal and practical issues to be dealt with. It is normal for the directors to meet to attend to these (although some matters may also require a decision by the shareholders). The issues to be considered may include approving any pre-incorporation expenditure and arranging for the company to reimburse the promoters.

Many of the other matters which the directors may need to consider are the same as those in relation to sole traders, ordinary partnerships and LLPs.

7.5.1 Appointing a chair

Many private companies have a chair who takes charge of directors' meetings and shareholders' meetings. **MA13** provides that the chair (referred to as the "chairman") has a second or **casting vote** at directors' meetings if votes on a decision are tied. This may not be appropriate in companies where all the participants have an equal interest in the company. In those companies, the members may adopt a special article disapplying **MA13**, or they may decide not to appoint a chair. In Samantha's company, on the other hand, Samantha holds 80 per cent of the shares, and it may be considered appropriate for her to be chair and to have a casting vote.

7.5.2 Bank account

The company is certain to want a bank account. Even if the company is taking over an existing unincorporated business, it will be necessary to open a new account in the company's own name, because the business's previous accounts will have been in the name(s) of the person or persons who owned the business before. The bank will usually specify the form of wording which the directors must use when they are deciding to open the account. This will include deciding who is allowed to sign on the company's behalf, and approving specimen signatures. It may also include a limit on the amount of money which any one person can withdraw from the account without a second signature.

7.5.3 Share capital

The company may have been formed with only one or two subscriber shares, particularly if it was a shelf company. If it was a shelf company, those shares will need to be transferred into the names of the intended shareholders. It may also be necessary to issue further new shares to the intended members, possibly for cash, or possibly in return for assets, such as the assets of an existing business.

For example, we have already seen in relation to Samantha's company that it could have been formed with a single subscriber, Samantha, who would take one share. Once the company is formed, it would be necessary to issue the remaining 199,999 shares to Samantha in return for the assets of her business, and 50,000 shares to Maja, in return for her cash investment.

7.5.4 Directors and secretary

It may also be necessary to appoint new directors, to include everyone who is intended to be a director. Again, this is particularly likely if the company was a shelf company – and in that situation the original directors will need to resign once the new directors have been appointed.

A shelf company is unlikely to have been formed with a company secretary. If one is required, they will need to be appointed at this stage.

7.5.5 Directors' service contracts

As you will see in **Chapter 9**, directors may be employees of the company. In that case, it is strongly advisable that they should have written service contracts, and these should be entered into after the company has been formed.

7.5.6 Accounting reference date

The **accounting reference date** (**ARD**) is the company's financial year end – the date to which the company's accounts are made up each year. When a new company is formed, its first ARD is the anniversary of the last day of the month in which it was incorporated. For example, the ARD of a company formed on 8 January 2023 will be 31 January. Its first set of annual accounts will be for the year ending 31 January 2024.

This may not suit the company, and so the directors may decide to change it.

7.5.7 Other matters to be dealt with if the company was a shelf company

As we have seen, if the company was a shelf company its name is unlikely to be suitable, and the directors may also wish to change its registered office. This can be done at this stage.

7.5.8 Business name

Even if the company's name does not need to be changed, the directors may decide at this point to adopt a business name.

7.5.9 Accountants and auditor

Just like an LLP, a company will need to file accounts in a specified format. Depending on the company's size, those accounts may need to be audited. The company will almost certainly wish to appoint accountants and, if its accounts will need to be audited, it is normal to appoint an auditor at this stage. The auditor is likely to be a member of the firm of accountants appointed by the company.

7.5.10 Company records

A company is required to keep extensive records – for example, records of directors' and shareholder meetings, and also registers of its shareholders and directors. It is the responsibility of the company's directors and other officers to maintain these records and keep them up to date, and failure to do so is a criminal offence.

It is normal to produce the records at the first directors' meeting, so that they can be satisfied that the necessary paperwork has been prepared and is ready to be updated as necessary.

NB Companies may elect to keep the required information about directors and members on the public register at Companies House instead of recording it in its own registers. This information will then be publicly available. See https://www.gov.uk/government/publications/company-registers/company-registers .

7.5.11 The company seal

A company's **seal** is a stamp containing a metal disc with the company's name engraved on it. It can be used to emboss the company's name on a document, as a way of authenticating the document, particularly in order to execute deeds.

There is no longer a requirement for a company to have a seal. If it does not, the company will use other procedures to authenticate documents and execute deeds. The advantage of having a seal is that the very act of applying it to a document concentrates the minds of the people involved – it may make them think harder about what they are doing.

If the company is to have a seal, it must be adopted by a decision of the directors. They usually decide to do this at the first directors' meeting.

7.5.12 Tax registration

A company pays **corporation tax** on its profits. The company will have been automatically registered for corporation tax with HMRC when it was incorporated. It will still be necessary to deal with registration for PAYE, national insurance and – depending on the nature and size of the company's business – VAT.

7.5.13 Disclosure of company details

Like LLPs, companies are subject to the disclosure requirements in the **Company, Limited Liability Partnership and Business (Names and Trading Disclosures) Regulations 2015**. The main requirements are similar to those which apply to LLPs. They include that:

(1) the company's registered name must be displayed at its registered office;

(2) on all business documents and websites, the company must disclose its registered name, its registered number and the address of its registered office;

(3) if the company names any director on its business documents (other than in the text of the document or as a signatory) or on its website, it must then give the names of all its directors.

The directors should therefore ensure that these requirements are complied with. If the company trades under a business name, they should also ensure that the company complies with the rules on disclosure of information in **ss1200–1206 CA 2006**.

7.5.14 Shareholders' agreement

The shareholders may choose to enter into an agreement containing further details about how the company is to be run. Many of these details could be included in the company's articles of association, but this has some disadvantages, including that:

- the articles can be changed by a specified majority of the shareholders, whereas (unless it provides otherwise) an agreement can be changed only with the agreement of **all** the parties;
- the articles are a public document, available for inspection at Companies House, whereas an agreement is private;
- an agreement between shareholders can also include other parties who are not shareholders – for example, lenders.

Such an agreement is often called a **shareholders' agreement** (even if some of the parties are not shareholders).

7.6 Public companies: minimum share capital and trading certificate

Like private companies, PLCs can be formed very simply. There is no minimum requirement for the formation of a PLC. However, **s763** provides that a PLC cannot do business unless its issued share capital is at least £50,000 (or the euro equivalent). Its issued share capital must be paid up to at least one-quarter of its nominal value (**s761**). So, if a PLC has issued share capital of £50,000, its shares must be paid up as to at least £12,500.

Before a PLC can do business, its directors must apply to the Registrar of Companies for a certificate confirming that these requirements have been complied with. This is something that the directors of a new PLC will want to do at an early stage.

Knowledge checks!

(1) Which of the following is a person of significant control in relation to Wilbury (Shoe Repairs) Ltd?

- (a) Safia owns 20 per cent of the voting rights in the company.
- (b) Johann has the right to appoint one director of the company. The company has four directors.
- (c) Tor has no shares in the company and is not a director but is married to Marian who owns 80 per cent of the voting shares and who always does what Tor says in relation to company decisions.

(2) A company promoter will always be liable for any pre-incorporation contracts which they sign. True or false?

- (a) True
- (b) False

7.7 Summary!

(1) Matters to be considered before forming a company include what articles of association are required, whether the company is to be a shelf company or tailor-made, who will be the shareholders and directors, what will be the share capital, whether a company secretary is required, where the registered office will be and what will be the company name.

(2) To form a company, Form IN01 is submitted to Companies House, together with the memorandum of association, articles of association (if the Model Articles are not being adopted without amendment) and the required fee. If all is in order, a certificate of incorporation will be issued.

(3) A company's promoters are fiduciaries and may be liable to account to the company for any profit made on contracts with the company when it was formed. Any contracts entered into by the promoters on behalf of the company before it is formed should expressly provide that they are entered into on behalf of the future company and that the promoter will not be liable on the contract.

(4) Once the company has been formed, the directors will need to meet to deal with post-incorporation matters. These will include most of the matters which arise in relation to sole traders, ordinary partnerships and LLPs, but there are a number of additional matters and a few other differences.

CHAPTER 8

Franchises and Buying and Selling Businesses

Aims of chapter!

This chapter will enable you to:

- Explain the nature of a franchise
- Describe the advantages and disadvantages of franchises
- Identify the key differences between an asset sale and a share sale
- Explain how an acquisition may be financed

- Describe the preliminary documentation for a business acquisition
- Identify the requirements of due diligence,
- Explain the purposes of warranties and disclosure
- Describe how the sale and purchase transaction is effected
- Draft a simple sale and purchase agreement
- Outline the tax implications of a sale and purchase, and
- Exchange and completion (including conditional completion)

8.1 Introduction

This chapter focusses on franchising and the acquisition of companies and businesses.

Franchising is used by businesses – **franchisors** – which have developed a business concept – say the format for a restaurant chain. The franchisors appoint **franchisees** who will set up their own businesses – restaurants, in this example – using the franchisor's business concept. The franchisor allows the franchisee to use their business concept in return for a fee. They may also sell goods to the franchisee – say, ingredients for the food sold by the restaurants, but possibly also décor and items such as waiters' uniforms – and/or provide services to them (say, restaurant design services, and developing menus). They will want to maintain close control over the quality of everything that the franchisees do, to preserve the reputation of their business concept.

Both private and public companies or their assets are bought and sold daily all over the world, and whilst there may be more regulatory requirements for a public company, the structure of the deal, the contract and commercial considerations are essentially the same. This is true irrespective of the size of the transaction, the value of the transaction or the parties involved.

In this chapter you will read about the process of buying (otherwise known as the acquisition) and selling (the disposal) a private limited company or its assets. You may also have heard of the term "merger" which involves the coming together of two commercial bodies, sharing resources and increasing their market share, and the term "takeover" which tends to apply to public companies, whereby the acquiring company buys a majority shareholding of another target company in order to take control over the company. These structures are outside the scope of this chapter.

The transactions throughout this chapter are between two parties; this is known as a private treaty transaction, as opposed to an auction sale, where there maybe multiple bidders for the company or its assets. We will also only look at transactions within the jurisdiction of England and Wales, as certain jurisdictions such as Germany and France are governed by civil codes, where additional rules and obligations apply. These include the concept of negotiating in good faith which, believe it or not, is not a concept we legally acknowledge or abide by in England and Wales.

There are many commercial reasons as to why corporations acquire businesses, such as corporate growth, diversification of products, increasing market share to name but a few – and despite recent global political and economic events including of course the pandemic, the rate of acquisitions and mergers globally has rocketed.

Practice link!

Proposed merger – Vodafone and Three

The proposed merger between the telecoms companies Vodafone and Three may have major implications for mobile users in the UK. The following *Guardian* article discusses the implications for competition and consumers:

https://www.theguardian.com/technology/2024/nov/05/what-would-a-merger-between-vodafone-and-three-mean-for-customers

8.2 Franchising

As discussed at the start of this chapter, franchising is an arrangement under which a franchisor allows a franchisee to use a business concept in return for a fee. The benefit for franchisors is that their franchisees will invest their own resources to expand the business. This can allow them to grow their business much more quickly than if they were relying on their own resources, but with less expenditure and without incurring direct liability to lenders, customers, staff and other suppliers.

In return, franchisees benefit from what they hope will be a successful business idea. If the franchise brand is already established, they also have the benefit of its goodwill. They will be supported by the franchisor during the start-up period, which is often the most difficult time for a new business. Because of all these advantages they may find it easier to access finance than if they were starting out completely on their own.

Activity!

Go to the Franchise UK website and review the Muffin Break Franchise at https://www.franchise-uk.co.uk/franchise/muffin-break-franchise/ .

What are the benefits of owning a Muffin Break franchise (other than lots of muffins!)?

8.2.1 How does franchising work?

There is no single answer to this question. The essence of franchising is that the franchisor permits the franchisee to use their business concept to set up an independent business. This will involve the franchisor granting the franchisee permission to use their intellectual property rights, usually by way of an intellectual property licence.

The franchisor may also provide services to the franchisee. These can range from staff training to designing the franchisee's retail outlet – and everything in between. The franchisor may supply goods to the franchisee as well. These can be one-off items – perhaps furniture for a restaurant – or regular supplies, perhaps of stock for sale, or restaurant ingredients.

Activity!

Review the blog on the Franchise UK website at https://www.franchise-uk.co.uk/franchise-news/ .

What is the advice on raising money to purchase a franchise?

What is the role of a franchise manager?

How does the franchisor make money from the arrangement? There is a wide range of possibilities. It is common for franchisees to pay an initial fee to join the franchise, followed by a regular payment, which may be calculated as a percentage of their sales or profits. The franchisee may also pay the franchisor for services or goods sourced from them.

8.2.2 Disadvantages

So why doesn't every business use franchising? It does bring disadvantages as well as benefits.

From the point of view of the franchisor, the biggest drawback is loss of control. The individual franchised businesses will be run by the franchisees, not the franchisor. The franchisor's main concern is to ensure consistency and quality. If franchisees provide poor service, this will adversely affect the franchisor's reputation and can damage the value of the entire franchise network. The franchisor therefore needs to ensure that there are sufficient control mechanisms in place.

Seen from the point of view of the franchisee, the main downside is a lack of autonomy. Any initiatives to improve the business format are likely to require the franchisor's approval, and the control mechanisms in the franchise agreement can even restrict the franchisee's options when dealing with day-to-day problems.

Also, if the business does well the benefit of the goodwill will accrue to the franchisor, not the franchisee. This also means that it will be difficult, if not impossible, for the franchisee to sell the business. Usually, the only way that a franchisee can benefit from selling a franchise is if the agreement allows it to transfer it to a new franchisee and the new franchisee pays for the goodwill that the old franchisee has built up. However, the agreement will always provide that the franchisor must first approve the new franchisee. Thus, the franchisor can always exercise a significant degree of control if the franchise is transferred, and this is likely to affect the value of the franchise.

8.2.3 Legal issues

A franchise agreement is likely to be a combination of several different types of agreement, including one or more intellectual property licences, an agreement to provide services to the franchisee and an agreement to distribute goods to the franchisee for onward sale.

The agreement is likely to contain restrictions on competition. For example, each franchisee may want the franchisor to agree not to appoint another franchisee within a specified geographical area, and in turn the franchisor may want to protect its other franchisees by requiring each of them to agree not to market the franchise products outside their allocated areas.

Restrictions on how franchisees can sell the franchise products may also be anti-competitive, particularly if they relate to the prices at which they can be sold. The parties therefore need to be alert to the impact of competition law on their agreement.

Another area of difficulty with franchises often arises where the franchised business does not perform as well as the parties expected. The franchised concept may have been misconceived – or the franchisee may not have implemented it in the way that the franchisor expected. In between these extremes there are any number of other possible reasons – for example, the franchisor may not have provided adequate training, or the goods or services supplied may have been inappropriate in some way. It is therefore important that the agreement contains provisions dealing with liability – particularly for potential misrepresentations by the franchisor, but also for other shortcomings in its implementation by either party.

Often the franchisor is in a stronger bargaining position if the franchise is well established. This gives rise to a risk that it will impose unfair terms on its franchisees.

Exclusions of liability for misrepresentation, for breach of written standard terms and for breach of the statutory implied terms relating to quality, etc. will all be subject to the reasonableness test under the **Misrepresentation Act 1967** or the **Unfair Contract Terms Act 1977**, and the parties' relative bargaining strengths will be taken into account when deciding whether they are reasonable.

The British Franchise Association (https://www.thebfa.org/) is a voluntary body which aims to establish ethical standards for franchising. Franchisors which are members are required to meet certain minimum standards. These include a requirement to operate a pilot operation to test its concept before the franchise is first launched and a requirement to provide initial and continuing training.

8.2.4 The franchise agreement

No two franchises are the same, and neither are any two franchise agreements. Most franchise agreements will contain at a minimum:

- a licence to use the necessary intellectual property rights. These are likely to consist of at least a registered trade mark (or the right to use the franchisor's name and goodwill and any other identifying marks, if they are not all registered). As is normal in a trade mark licence, the agreement should ensure that ownership of all goodwill in the business remains with the franchisor. There may also be licences of copyright and/or design rights, and conceivably even patents;

- a duty to keep any information supplied confidential;
- provision to allow the franchisor to exercise the necessary control. This is usually done by requiring the franchisee to comply with a **franchise manual** (which the franchisor can amend). The agreement should specify what will happen if the franchisee fails to comply – including termination of the franchise in an appropriate case; and
- provision for payment of fees, either one-off and/or recurring.

Most franchise agreements will then also include:

- provisions for the supply of goods and/or services;
- initial and continuing training, where this is relevant to the franchise;
- restrictions on competition;
- provisions regulating the liability of both parties (exactly what these say will depend on the parties' bargaining strength); and
- provisions on termination. These may allow the franchisor to take over the franchisee's business, so as to be able to continue to benefit from it.

8.3 Transaction structure

What do we mean by an asset sale (often referred to as a business sale) or a share sale, and what factors affect the decision to structure the deal as a share or asset sale?

If a transaction is structured as a share sale, it means that the entire company is sold with all of its liabilities, such as on-going litigation or debts owed to third parties, and all of its assets, plant, machinery and properties, for example. The buyer will also acquire everything that the target company owns, including any subsidiary companies. The transaction revolves around the transferring of shares owned by the shareholder(s) to the new owner(s) of the company. On the face of it, the transaction is relatively straightforward – consideration is paid for the shares and the company has new owners. To those within the company, and to a greater extent external third parties, there will not be a noticeable difference.

Businesses can and do sell individual assets on a regular basis, but when we refer to an asset sale throughout this chapter, we are referring to the sale of enough individual assets, including goodwill, within the business, to enable the business to continue to trade as a going concern post completion. In other words, the new owners will carry on running the same business that was in existence, prior to the sale. This could be a trading arm or division of the company or in fact the entire business of the company, leaving only an empty shell of a company behind.

There are many factors that will affect the decision-making process of the parties as to whether they choose to buy or sell a company or just its business. The most beneficial tax position tends to be the biggest driver of a commercial transaction of this nature, but of course the bargaining power of each party will ultimately dictate the structure of the deal.

8.3.1 The parties to the transaction

In a share sale, the seller(s) is (1) the owner of the company, (2) the shareholder – that may be several individuals, or a single company or a combination of the two. The transaction will be between the purchaser and the shareholder(s).

In an asset sale, the seller is the owner(s) of the assets. If you are dealing with an unincorporated entity or a partnership, that may be an individual (and others) or the partnership.

However throughout this chapter, when we consider asset sales the seller will be the company itself. As such, the transaction will be between the purchaser of the assets (the buyer) and the target company (the seller).

Each party to the transaction will have a team of professional advisers, such as lawyers, accountants and various commercial parties.

The following diagram is an example of a share sale and an asset sale, before and after the transactions.

Share sale

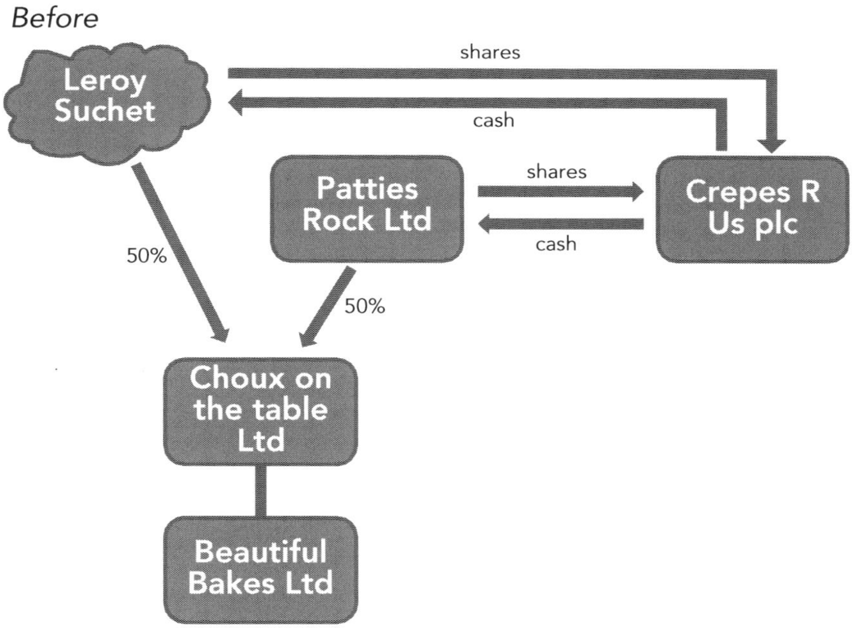

Figure 8.3.1a

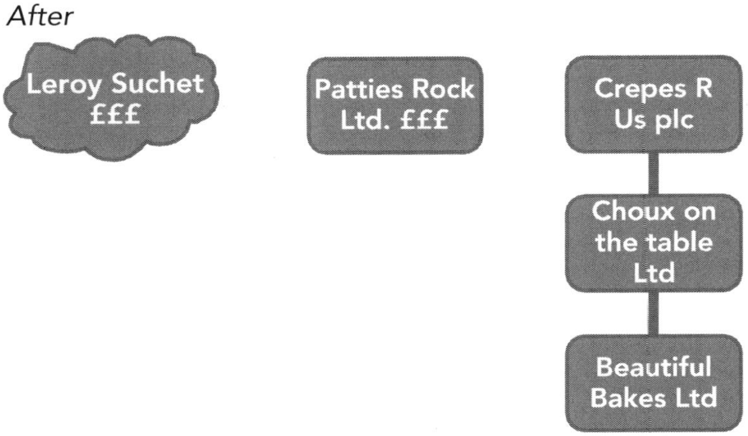

Figure 8.3.1b

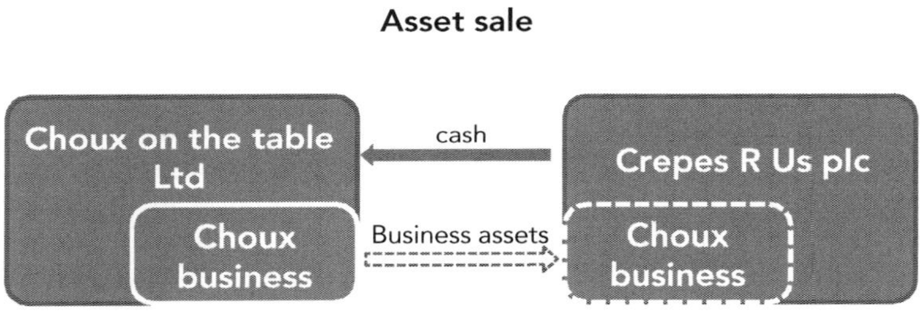

Figure 8.3.1c

In figures 8.3.1a and 8.3.1b you can see that in the share sale, the shareholders Leroy Suchet and the company Patties Rock Ltd sell their 100 per cent shareholding in the company (often referred to as the target) Choux on the table Ltd to Crepes R Us plc, who pays the agreed price to the shareholders. Once the transaction is complete, Crepes R Us plc will own a new subsidiary company, and everything that it owns including its subsidiary company Beautiful Bakes Ltd.

In the asset sale (figure 8.3.1c) the actual company, Choux on the table Ltd, is selling all of the assets that make up its business to the buyer Crepes R Us plc, which will pay the requisite consideration directly to Choux on the table Ltd. Post transaction, Crepes R Us plc will not have a new company but a new business that it must integrate within its existing company structure.

There are many differences between a share sale and asset sale and consequently numerous advantages and disadvantages for both the buyer and seller. Many of the factors set out in the following section will have been considered by the parties long before a lawyer is instructed.

8.3.2 Differences between a share sale and an asset sale

	Share sale	Asset sale
Seller	Shareholder(s) of target company will sell entire shareholding	Company which owns and operates the business
Due diligence	Investigation of entire target company and everything it owns by buyer	Investigation of assets that buyer wishes to acquire
Liabilities	All liabilities remain with the target company	The buyer has the option to leave all liabilities behind. It would need to state in the acquisition agreement which liabilities it chooses to take on
Employees	The target company is the employer; this remains the same post completion. The employees will not be affected	**Transfer of Undertakings (Protection of Employment) Regulations 2006** (**TUPE**) may apply. Buyer will not be able to leave workforce behind

	Share sale	Asset sale
Contractual arrangements	Existing contracts remain the same and automatically move with the company. The only issue is if contracts have change of control (ownership) clauses, which may give the contracting party the right to terminate the contract if the company is sold	Each contract will need to be individually transferred; this can trigger assignment/consent issues and contracts may need to be novated or renegotiated
Tax	VAT is not applicable Stamp duty for sale of shares: 0.5% of total consideration (price) Corporate seller is liable to pay corporation tax (subject to certain exemptions and reliefs) Individual sellers are liable to pay capital gains tax (subject to certain exemptions and reliefs)	VAT is applicable unless the transfer of the business is exempt because under the **Value Added Tax Act 1994** because it is being sold as a going concern Stamp duty land tax will apply – rates depend on the value of the land – see https://www.gov.uk/stamp-duty-land-tax/nonresidential-and-mixed-rates

8.4 Financing an acquisition

There are two main methods of funding an acquisition, unless of course the buyer has surplus cash reserves for this purpose. First, a buyer will tend to rely on debt, either in the form of **debt** securities, an example of such would be by issuing bonds in itself to the public, or by taking out loans. Second, the alternative method would be by raising **equity**, which is where the purchasing company issues new shares in itself to either existing shareholders or brand-new investors, or even to the seller itself. This is known as a share for share exchange, which tends to occur more in companies that are listed on a recognised stock exchange such as the London Stock Exchange, because those shares are more marketable, or easier to sell. There are statutory restrictions in place that prevent a private limited company offering shares out to the public, and so it is more common for a public company whose shares are listed to issues shares in itself in order to fund an acquisition.

Terminology!

Consideration is a term used in Contract Law which means the price of a contract. This may, of course, be a payment of cash but it can include handing over other assets, such as shares in the seller's company.

8.4.1 Cash versus paper consideration

This is commonly referred to as cash or paper consideration; paper being in the form of shares or loan notes. If we return to the share sale (as set out at **8.3.1**), the board of Crepes R Us plc ("Crepes") will have considered which form of finance it will use to fund the purchase of Choux on the table Ltd. The selling shareholders, Leroy Suchet and Patties Rock Ltd, have set the price for the entire share capital of Choux on the table Ltd at £5 million. When deciding whether to take out a loan or issue more shares in itself, the board of directors of Crepes will need to take the following factors into consideration:

- What is the most tax-efficient method of funding the acquisition?
- The cost of a loan, what are interest rates like at the moment?

- What sort of security can it offer to a lender?
- Will Crepes' credit rating enable it to take out a loan?
- How will further debt affect its gearing ratio (a comparison of borrowings to shareholders funds – if too high it may put future investors off!)?
- Is there a market for its shares?
- Will its own shareholders approve the issuance of more shares – this will dilute the value of their own shareholdings?
- Do Crepes' articles require the shares to be issued to the existing shareholders first?
- Will Leroy Suchet and Patties Rock Ltd accept shares in Crepes as consideration?

Alternatively, if the buyer in a transaction is a company (as is the case in the above example) and it finds itself struggling to raise the requisite funds, the sellers may be willing to accept loans notes (bonds) from the buyer. A loan note is in its simplest form an IOU, a document that sets out the terms of the buyer's debt to the sellers. It enables the buyer to pay off the price of the target company in instalments. The sellers will agree a reasonable rate of interest and a time period in which they must be fully paid. This may be beneficial to the sellers as it will enable them (particularly if they are an individual such as Leroy Suchet) to pay tax in instalments, as and when they cash in the loan notes.

8.4.2 Earnouts

If the buyer is in a particularly strong bargaining position, it may agree to pay part of the consideration on completion of the deal and the rest of the consideration at some point in the future (say two or three years' time) when the company has hit a certain level of profit. The outstanding amount is known as deferred consideration. This amount tends to be a multiplied figure or a percentage of the gross profit achieved by the business, which makes it worthwhile to the sellers. This scheme would be tempting to an individual shareholder such as Leroy, particularly if he was also a director who wanted to remain working for the target company. This deferred consideration would act as a great incentive to ensure the target performs well.

8.5 Preliminary documentation

There are many stages to an acquisition:

- the early stages where each party is considering the structure of the deal and how it might be financed;
- the preliminary documentation – confidentiality agreement, heads of agreement;
- due diligence where the company/business is investigated;
- negotiating the sale and purchase agreement;
- exchange and completion; and
- post-completion matters.

As we have already looked at the structure of the deal and how it might be financed, let's move on to the preliminary documentation.

The easiest way to learn about acquisitions is to work through an actual transaction; as such, from this point on we will refer to the scenario details set out at **8.3.1**.

Law in context!

You have now received instructions from your clients, Leroy Suchet and Patties Rock Ltd, which is run by Leroy's spouse, Yolanda Suchet referred to collectively as the "Suchets". Your firm has carried out the client conflict checks and as both parties own an equal shareholding of 50 per cent, you have been authorised to act for both parties.

The Suchets wish to sell the entire share capital of the target company Choux on the table Ltd ("the Target"), which includes its subsidiary company Beautiful Bakes Ltd ('Beautiful Bakes'). The Target specialises in upmarket pastries delivered to your door and saw a phenomenal uptake in sales and profitability recently, largely due to the global pandemic. The Suchets now want to sell the Target to focus more on their family business Patties Rock Ltd. They are selling the Target for £5 million in cash and would like to complete the transaction as soon as possible.

You have checked the provisions of the **Financial Services and Markets Act 2000**, to ensure you are not in breach of **s19**:

> *No person may carry on a regulated activity in the United Kingdom unless he is:*
>
> *(a) an authorised person; or*
>
> *(b) an exempt person.*

You are also not in breach of **s21** of the Act, as you have not carried out any form of financial promotion in order to incentivise others to purchase the shares. You have been instructed that this is a private treaty sale and the sellers have already found their buyer, Crepes R Us plc.

8.5.1 Confidentiality agreement

The first of the preliminary documents that must be considered is the confidentiality agreement, sometimes referred to as an NDA – meaning a non-disclosure agreement. This document is key to any commercial transaction of this nature. During the course of negotiating an acquisition, a great deal of information, sometimes sensitive information, relating to the target company, will pass between the parties – particularly, when the buyer starts its investigation of the target as part of its due diligence exercise. The target must be protected, as not only will the selling party and the target itself lose out if their confidential information is leaked to the public or a competitor prior to the deal, but the potential purchaser of the target will also be affected as the value of the target may diminish.

In the early stages of the negotiations, the sellers will even want the existence of the deal to be kept confidential, as any leak can have detrimental effects on the target's workforce and potentially their customers. As a result of this the parties will want to put a confidentiality agreement in place at the earliest possible stage. The target should also be a party to this deal, since ultimately it will be the body that has the most to lose and must therefore have the right to take action against the party who is in breach.

The parties to the transaction will enter into a confidentiality agreement that is fairly standard in terms of structure. There will be a clear "definitions" clause dictating exactly what the selling party considers to be confidential information, such as, using our example, recipes, customer lists, intellectual property (IP) etc. This definition should not be too wide, and it should specifically exclude any information that is already in the public domain. There should be a clear purpose for the confidential information and clauses which set out exactly how the information can be used, and which parties are authorised to do so.

There will possibly be a non-solicitation provision. If the potential seller reveals, for example, a list of its key clients or allows the buyer access to some of its senior employees, the buyer cannot, at this stage, steal those customers or employees, and there should also be clear and unequivocal consequences for any breach of the terms of confidentiality set out in the agreement.

Most standard confidentiality agreements will have a provision that states that all confidential information must be returned and/or destroyed after a certain period of time or upon request of the seller, should the deal not go ahead. It may contain a remedy of liquidated damages (a monetary value placed upon a breach of the terms of the agreement). However, because it can be quite difficult to estimate just how much damage a breach of confidentiality can inflict upon the injured party, more and more confidentiality agreements will provide for an order of specific performance, where the courts can order the party in breach to perform a specific action. This is particularly useful if the seller knows that the buyer is about to release/use some form of confidential information. The courts can order the buyer to cease all activity and prevent the breach from occurring.

Lastly, there will be a jurisdiction clause as the parties would want the agreement to be subject to the jurisdiction of choice, for example, England and Wales.

Crepes and the Suchets in our scenario will sign an agreement stipulating what information should be protected, who the parties are, and who is authorised to use the information and for a specific purpose. It will contain amongst other things: a provision that the deal will be kept confidential; non-solicitation provisions; financial and/ or injunctive relief available for any breach of its terms; a provision stating how long the information should be kept confidential for – indefinitely is not always appropriate or enforceable; and lastly, a jurisdiction clause stating that the terms of the agreement will be subject to the exclusive jurisdiction of the courts of England and Wales.

8.5.2 Heads of agreement

You may have heard of the terms "heads of agreement", "heads of terms", "letters of intent", "memorandum of understanding". Essentially, they all mean the same thing; a general, commercial document that sets out the basic commercial terms of a proposed deal. This document can provide the parties with a firm basis upon which to negotiate the actual sale and purchase documentation. By setting out the general scope of the deal at this stage, the parties can avoid any major misunderstandings at a later date as to the structure of the deal, the method of consideration, and the general purpose of the transaction.

Note that the heads of agreement (HOA), acts as no more than a guide between the parties; it is not meant to be a legally binding document. In fact, many acquisitions will proceed without any form of HOA and go straight to negotiating the sale and purchase agreement, as this saves time and money. More worryingly, the parties may sign a "standard" HOA, which has not been reviewed by a lawyer, which could lead to the parties being tied into a deal that is not necessarily what either party envisaged.

Nonetheless, in our transaction our client, the Suchets, wish to enter into a HOA, as they want the commercial scope of the deal set out in one document from the outset. One of the key issues of the HOA is its non-binding nature. The HOA is, as mentioned, not on the whole a legally binding document, and Crepes at this stage certainly would not want to be obliged to purchase the target company before it has carried out its due diligence. Therefore, the document can be drafted in such a way as to ensure that only certain provisions, which the parties require legal protection for, are legally binding. For example, both parties would want the provisions of the HOA and the deal itself kept confidential (as set out at **8.5.1**). The parties will probably sign a separate confidentiality agreement, but they may also wish to set out some basic terms of confidentiality within the HOA.

By this stage, Crepes will have already spent a great deal of time and money researching the target to ensure it is a good commercial deal. Once it has indicated to the Suchets that it wishes to purchase the target it will not want them to negotiate the sale of the target with any other interested third party, not at least until it has carried out its internal investigation of the target and its due diligence exercise. Whilst it is carrying this out, it will want a period of exclusivity, and it will also want this provision to be legally binding.

Under English law a period of exclusivity, where the selling party will not negotiate with a third a party for a period of time, is legally acceptable as long as the wording of the clause is very carefully drafted and is sufficiently certain. In ***Walford v Miles [1992]*** it was held that in order for an exclusivity clause to be valid it must include certain elements:

- It must be a negative obligation and must be worded so that the buyer will not negotiate with any other party. This is known as a "lock out" clause. The HOA cannot state that the seller will only negotiate with the proposed buyer as this would be a positive obligation, or an agreement to agree. This would be considered unenforceable due to a lack of certainty.
- The clause should contain a definite time period. The exclusivity cannot continue indefinitely, and must be for an appropriate period of time, subject to the size and nature of the deal.
- The obligation on the seller not to negotiate with another party should be supported by good and valid consideration. This can be in any form. It can be a nominal sum of £1. It could be in relation to a non-monetary commitment between the parties, for example, the buyer's commitment to carry out due diligence. The document could even be signed as a deed in certain circumstances.

The exclusivity clause may also contain a provision for costs/break fees should one party breach the terms of the exclusivity provision and/or end the negotiations prematurely.

An informal HOA for our deal may look something along the lines of the following:

Subject to Contract

Choux on the table Ltd
Battenberg Lane London
E8 8TE

The Directors:
Crepes R Us plc 245
Flambe Street
Berkshire
BK2 8DL

Strictly Private & Confidential

Dear Jean,

Re: Choux on the table Ltd

Thank you for expressing an interest in the proposed acquisition of the entire share capital of Choux on the table Ltd (the "Target") including the shares of its subsidiary company Beautiful Bakes Ltd (the "Transaction"). The following sets out the proposed commercial terms of the Transaction between your company Crepes R Us plc, (the "Buyer") and ourselves Leroy Suchet and Patties Rock Ltd (the "Sellers").

With the exception of clauses 4, 6 and 7, these Heads of Agreement are not intended to be legally binding and merely represent the intention of the parties to enter into the Transaction.

Principal Terms

(1) The Buyer shall, subject to the terms and conditions set out below, acquire the Target at completion of the Transaction for a purchase price of £5 m, exclusive of VAT (the "Purchase Price").

(2) The Share Sale and Purchase Agreement will contain Warranties and Indemnities on a joint and several basis, as are usual for a transaction of this nature.

(3) The parties will negotiate a Share Sale and Purchase Agreement and other appropriate legal documentation.

Exclusivity

(4) In consideration of the Buyer carrying out its due diligence exercise and incur- ring further costs in preparing the Share Sale and Purchase Agreement we, the Sellers, undertake that we will not, for a period of [3 months] from the date of these Heads of Agreement, approach, entertain and negotiate with any other person with a view to entering into a transaction which would preclude or materially restrict or delay the Transaction.

Due Diligence

(5) We agree that the Buyer's lawyers, accountants and appropriate professional advisers may have full access to our Data Room and the accounts of the Target for the past five years.

Confidentiality

(6) These Heads of Agreement are without prejudice to the confidentiality agreement signed by the parties to this Heads of Agreement on [date].

(7) These Heads of Agreement shall be governed by and construed in accordance with English law. Each of the parties submit to the exclusive jurisdiction of the English courts.

We look forward to receiving a signed copy of these Heads of Agreement enclosed within this letter by return.

Yours sincerely,

Leroy Suchet CEO

Choux on the table Ltd, and Yolanda

Suchet

Signing for and on behalf of Patties

Rock Ltd

8.6 Due diligence and disclosure

The buyer will at this stage have signed a confidentiality agreement and possibly heads of agreement similar to our example (at **8.5.2**). However, before it starts to incur costs that relate to the drafting of the sale and purchase agreement (in a private acquisition, the buyer usually prepares the first draft), it will want to carry out a full investigation into the business, or in our example, the company that it intends to purchase. This is referred to as due diligence. The main objective of due diligence is for the buyer to ascertain whether or not the proposed acquisition is a good and potentially profitable commercial investment, and on what terms this investment should be made. As mentioned above, there is very little statutory or common law protection for a buyer in a commercial acquisition in England and Wales. The principle of "*caveat emptor*" – let the buyer beware, means that most of the risk lies with the buyer. As such, the buyer starts to effectively protect itself by reallocating some of that risk back to the seller at the due diligence stage of the transaction. What the buyer uncovers during this exercise will determine the price it is willing to pay for the business or company and what contractual protections it requires, or in fact if it should cut its losses and walk away from the deal.

The due diligence exercise whether it pertains to an asset sale or a share sale is very similar in structure, except for the fact that in a share sale, it will be more extensive, lengthy and therefore more costly as the buyer must investigate every aspect of the company – and everything it owns. In contrast, in an asset sale only the assets that the buyer wishes to purchase require investigation.

Another aspect of due diligence that is particularly relevant to our example is that the buyer, particularly one that is a publicly listed company, may discover at this early stage whether the deal will require any regulatory consents or approvals.

Due diligence can be carried out by a questionnaire (typical in a private treaty sale and purchase) that is sent to the seller by the buyer. It will contain a great many general questions that relate to every aspect of the target company, and some questions may relate to the sellers themselves. Alternatively, the seller can create a data room, which is more often than not a virtual data room. This is typical of an auction sale, where the seller is far more in control. The seller will, populate the "room" with information relating to the target that it anticipates the prospective buyer will be interested in (and what it chooses to reveal at this stage of the transaction).

There are three main areas of due diligence: legal, financial and commercial. We shall look at each area in turn.

8.6.1 Legal due diligence

In the context of the deal in our example, a private treaty share sale, Crepes' lawyer would send a comprehensive due diligence questionnaire to the Suchets, asking them to provide a lot of information. This may start with corporate housekeeping by requesting information relating to the target's statutory books, minutes and other information that may not be logged at Companies House (an independent search of the records held at Companies House would be carried out by Crepes in any event). It would also wish to see the register of members to ensure the Suchets have the right to actually sell the shares of the Target. (It should be noted that any reference to the target regarding the due diligence exercise shall include its subsidiary company Beautiful Bakes, as the Buyer will need to investigate that company too.)

Crepes would enquire, for example, about any litigation, arbitration or mediation, pending or otherwise that the Target may be involved in. Any serious litigation could have catastrophic consequences for the future trade and reputation of the target company that has just been purchased. For example, if the target in our scenario has produced meat patties, that were contaminated with a severe strain of bacteria causing sickness or even fatalities amongst its more vulnerable customers, that will stay with the Target post completion. It will be left with the target to pay damages and clear up any reputational damage, which would indirectly have a negative effect on the value of the Target that Crepes has just purchased, unless it is addressed by contractual protections in the form of warranties and or indemnities.

The questionnaire would most certainly focus on any key contracts and whether there are any onerous provisions or rights of termination within them – more particularly, any change of control (ownership) provisions that would entitle a third-party client to terminate that particular contract upon the sale of the target. This is relevant in a share sale as the target will ultimately have new owners. In an asset sale, any pertinent contracts would need to be assigned or novated to the new company, which has absorbed the business into its own company structure.

Any data protection issues will be investigated, as well as employee matters, for example, any key directors' service contracts will need to be scrutinised. Pensions are also a huge area of concern for a buyer in a share sale. If there are any final salary pensions in place that are in deficit, by purchasing the target it could trigger a **s75 Pensions Act 1995** liability, which may mean that the newly purchased target must contribute to a deficit in a pension scheme it is no longer a part of, which could indirectly cost the buyer millions of pounds.

8.6.2 Financial due diligence

Crepes should also ensure that its accountants carry out a thorough financial due diligence exercise. This will involve requesting the accounts of the target as well as information relating to its margins, profitability, trading history in order to analyse past financial performance and produce future profitability projections. The target's tax position will also be important here, as Crepes will not want to be responsible for any tax owed by the target prior to completion. The target's capital allowances will also be examined.

Pensions may also need to be investigated to ensure that outstanding liabilities for an final salary pensions are identified.

8.6.3 Commercial due diligence

This area of investigation can be as wide or as narrow as the parties require. It can involve investigation of any properties that the target may own and any intellectual property (IP) rights (which could also form part of the legal due diligence exercise). Operational strategies can be examined here as well as insurance policies, any commercial agreements that are between the target and other subsidiary companies within the sellers' group, environmental issues and any aspect of the target that affects its day-to-day trade.

In our scenario, contracts with suppliers, IP rights (recipes, know-how etc.), assets used in the baking process and employees will all be covered in the due diligence questionnaire.

The Suchets are under no obligation to answer every question on the questionnaire, but any omissions will more likely than not lead to further, more specific queries from Crepes and can prolong the entire exercise. Once Crepes' lawyer has received the completed questionnaire, it will produce a full or limited due diligence report for its client, who will use the information to start negotiating the contractual terms of the share sale and purchase agreement, which again usually comes from the buyer's lawyers in a private treaty transaction. The information gleaned may also cause Crepes to renegotiate the price for the target, or even abandon the deal entirely.

8.6.4 Warranties, indemnities and disclosure

We must now consider the purpose and nature of warranties and indemnities and how they help to reallocate the overall risk incurred by the purchaser in any acquisition.

Once Crepes has completed its due diligence exercise, it will have a fairly good understanding of the target and its true value. It is at this stage the parties – in our scenario, Crepes' lawyers – will begin to draft the share sale and purchase agreement (SPA). The most heavily negotiated part of the SPA are the warranties and indemnities. They can be so lengthy in nature, that rather than being set out in the main operative part of the SPA, they will usually be found in a schedule to the SPA.

In a share sale such as ours, Crepes is buying the entire target company, its assets (including its subsidiary Beautiful Bakes) and its liabilities, and as mentioned, it has very little statutory or common law protection (in an asset sale, statutes such as the **Sale of Goods Act 1979** may in certain circumstances afford the buyer some level of protection for the assets purchased). We have looked at one method Crepes can use to protect itself, which is finding out as much as it can about the target via due diligence, but this is not enough by itself. Crepes will want contractual protections in place which give it the right to some form of financial redress if the target is not quite what it thought it was.

(1) Warranties

One form of contractual protection is via a series of warranties. A warranty is a contractual statement of fact about the condition of the target company or business, at a certain point in time. If this statement is found to be untrue for whatever reason post completion, it gives the buyer the right to sue the seller for breach of contract which would give rise to a claim for damages to recover any diminution of the target's value. This is subject to any exclusions and or limitations the seller has managed to negotiate on its own behalf. As such, warranties serve two main purposes:

- to provide the buyer with the right to sue the seller if any of the warranties are untrue, which cause a reduction in the target company's value; and
- to provide the buyer with a means of eliciting further information about the target from the buyer. The seller will invariably disclose to the buyer any ongoing issues that it is aware of within the target that might render any warranty untrue, as this will limit the extent of the seller's liability. We shall discuss this in detail shortly.

Warranty claims in general are quite rare in acquisitions. They are expensive, time consuming and it can prove to be very difficult from the buyer's perspective to quantify loss caused to the value of its company, particularly if the damage is reputational. Therefore, the second "purpose" of a warranty is its most important function.

(2) **Indemnities**

An indemnity is a form of financial redress on a pound for pound basis if a specific liability is identified, which may occur in the future. The party in receipt of the indemnity will be reimbursed for any debt it has incurred as a result of this specific liability arising. For example, if the target is being sued and proceedings are not complete prior to completion, the buyer will require an indemnity stating that any sums paid out in relation to this litigation, including costs – if this has been agreed, will be reimbursed by the seller to the buyer, without the parties having to thrash it out in court, and more importantly without the need for the buyer to mitigate its losses.

Indemnities are often the preferred method of redress for the buyer, particularly where a warranty claim may not provide the buyer with an adequate remedy, that is, the actual value of the company has not been reduced. They are often used in areas where there is a clear identifiable risk. In our scenario, we looked at an example of pending mass litigation, but potential IP infringements or product liability issues, monies owed to the company or even environmental risks, are also areas that lend themselves well to indemnities.

When Crepes' lawyer sends the first draft of the SPA over to the Suchets, it will contain some specific indemnities and a raft of general warranties about the overall state of the target. As the target is in the food industry, the warranties will relate to key areas such as:

- title to the shares;
- compliance with industry specific regulations/legislation;
- IP;
- litigation;
- commercial contracts;
- employees/pensions; and
- accounts/tax.

An example of some warranties in the SPA for this deal are as follows:

> The Sellers warrant and represent to the Buyer that:
>
> 1.1 "The Target and its subsidiary company Beautiful Bakes are not engaged in any litigation, criminal or arbitration proceedings whether actual, pending or threatened or any other type of dispute whether of a formal or informal nature."
>
> Or
>
> 5.2 "The Target and its subsidiary company Beautiful Bakes each own or has a right to use all patents, trademarks, copyrights, registered designs, trade or business names or any other intellectual property right required in connection with the conduct of its business and does not thereby infringe any intellectual property rights of any third party."

As there are two sellers in our scenario, Crepes would insist on being able to claim against both parties, so it would ensure within its drafting of the SPA that the Suchets' obligations and therefore their liability is on a joint and several basis. This means that if there is a breach of warranty Crepes may take action against Leroy Suchet and/or Patties Rock Ltd for the full amount of loss. The Suchets can agree amongst themselves how they will share that liability.

It is at this point that the risk allocation game really begins. When the Suchets receive the first draft of the SPA from Crepes, and it contains numerous draft warranties, the Suchets will want to push back on that risk by watering down those warranties. Using the example set out above, the Suchets may not be aware of any potential claims or pending or threatened litigation. An employee that has burnt themself in the staff kitchen with hot tea supplied by the target, who shouts "I'm going to sue Choux on the table!" could be regarded as a threat, even if they have no real intention of suing their workplace. Alternatively, a registered patent or licence might have just expired, and this may go unnoticed by the target for months. In order to protect themselves further the Suchets would make the following amendments:

> The Sellers warrant to the Buyer that:
>
> 1.1 "So far as the Sellers are aware, the Target and its subsidiary company Beautiful Bakes are not engaged in any actual litigation, criminal or arbitration proceedings."
>
> Or
>
> 5.2 "To the best of the Sellers' knowledge, the Target and its subsidiary company Beautiful Bakes each own or has a right to use all patents, trademarks, copyrights, registered designs, trade or business names or any other intellectual property right required in connection with the conduct of its business and as far as the Sellers are aware, do not thereby infringe any intellectual property rights of any third party."

The Suchets' lawyers will attempt to water down as many warranties as possible. There are some that Crepes will not accept, such as ownership of the shares of the target, some it may concede on, and some that Crepes may push back on by inserting wording along the lines of "having made all reasonable and careful enquiry of [directors/heads of departments etc.]" or ensuring that the Suchets use their "best endeavours" whilst making these enquiries.

8.6.5 Disclosure

The Suchets will ultimately want to reduce or in fact eliminate the risk that is now back in their court. One of the principal methods of doing this is via a process known as disclosure. One of the most important function of a warranty is to provide the buyer with as much information about the target as possible. The benefit of this to the Suchets is that once Crepes has knowledge of an issue that might potentially render a warranty untrue, that knowledge will limit its right to claim for breach of that warranty post completion of the deal. The 'disclosure' will qualify the warranty, so the Suchets will generally want to disclose as much information as they can regarding any issue that may qualify a warranty to avoid being sued. The consequence of that is they run the risk of Crepes or any buyer negotiating a reduction in price or even walking away at quite a late stage in the negotiation; this tends to still be preferable to a claim post completion.

So, what would this disclosure exercise look like in practice? We know that the warranties will form a schedule to the main operative parts of the sale and purchase agreement. Instead of going through that list of warranties and providing any information that might qualify each relevant warranty, the seller's lawyer will put together a disclosure letter, with a bundle of evidence attached to it. The letter will have a front end and a back end to it. The front end will contain a list of general disclosures relating to information that is easily accessible to the buyer and therefore the buyer will be deemed to have knowledge about any such information on the target company for example, held at Companies House, or information held at the Land Registry or any public register. If the seller is shrewd enough, it may try to include any information the buyer has discovered via its own due diligence exercise, or state that any information relating to the target that is in the public domain is considered to be disclosed to the buyer, which can arguably qualify any number of warran ties and prevent the buyer from suing the seller – remember the principle, "let the buyer beware!" If the buyer accepts general disclosures of this nature, it will include anything on the internet that relates to the target. The idea behind the concept of disclosure is once you know or have knowledge of a matter relating to the company you are about to buy, and that information proves that one of the warranties is untrue, you cannot sue the selling party for breach of warranty! The buyer must always ensure that it can check these sources of information, which means a seller should always be able to verify the information contained within that source. If the buyer is willing to accept information held on a public register as being disclosed to it, then it should ensure that the search is narrowed down to specific dates and any reference to the "public domain" should be deleted in its entirety as being too wide.

The back end of the letter will contain disclosures that relate to specific warranties. Using our previous warranties as an example:

> 1.1 "So far as the Sellers are aware, the Target and its subsidiary company Beautiful Bakes are not engaged in any actual litigation, criminal or arbitration proceedings."

The specific entry in the disclosure letter may be something along the lines of:

> Warranty 1.1 – The Target has been sent a "letter before action" received on [date], from an employee who suffered severe burns in the staff canteen etc.

And with regard to the IP warranty:

> Warranty 5.2 – The Target's subsidiary has received a letter regarding a possible infringement of an IP right that relates to the design of a particular cake.

The disclosure letter would have a bundle of documents attached to it providing evidence to support each disclosure. This would include the letter before action from the employee and any communication from the third party alleging infringement of IP rights, which can result in a huge number of documents. Two identical copies of the disclosure letter and bundle of evidence should be made, and both the seller and buyer should have a signed copy at completion.

Case law has shown us that the standard of disclosure that the parties contractually agree to is crucial. Below is an example of a high level of disclosure agreed:

> The Sellers warrant and represent to the Buyer that except as fully, fairly, clearly and accurately disclosed, (with sufficient details to identify the nature and scope of the matter disclosed) in or under the disclosure letter, each Warranty is true, accurate and not misleading as at the date of this agreement.

The buyer is in a very good position here as this wording compels the seller to be very clear in its disclosures and will mean that any vague or general disclosures (such as "here are the accounts, see for yourself if there are any major accounting issues") will not meet with this high standard and this may not preclude a buyer from making a successful claim for breach of any warranty about the financial position of that company.

Conversely, the parties might agree a very low standard of disclosure such as:

> The Sellers warrant and represent to the Buyer that, except as disclosed, each Warranty is true, accurate and not misleading as at the date of this agreement.

In this example, the sellers will be in a strong position and would not have to specifically point out any financial discrepancies. They could simply disclose the accounts, for example, and let the buyer decipher what the issue is.

Similarly, the buyer's knowledge of an issue that may render a warranty untrue may prevent it from bringing a claim for breach of warranty, but only if the agreement states this.

A lawyer's advice to the seller in a transaction of this nature should, for the most part be "Disclose! Disclose! Disclose!"

8.6.6 Further protective provisions

There are many other ways in which the parties can protect themselves in an acquisition, for example:

- restrictive covenants;
- vendor protection provisions; and
- entire agreement clauses.

8.6.6.1 Restrictive covenants

Restrictive covenants must protect a legitimate business interest and be reasonable in terms of duration and geographical breadth. In the context of acquisitions, they are there to protect the target business or company, so the buyer will rely heavily on these provisions to prevent the seller from, amongst other things, setting itself up in direct competition with the target company or business within a short distance of its location. Restrictive covenants will also be used to protect the target's customer lists and prevent the seller from attempting to lure some of the target's employees back into the seller's group of companies, with better employment packages.

8.6.6.2 Vendor protection clauses

The main purpose of vendor protection provisions is to provide limitations to the liability faced by the seller in an acquisition if there was a breach of warranty claim or even potentially a claim under the tax deed or an indemnity, post completion. For example, the seller may place time limits on the length of time that it is liable to the buyer for any claim relating to the sale of the business/company. Many sale and purchase agreements will have a general time limit (long stop date) of possibly two to three years post completion for any and all claims under the agreement, with the exception of claims relating to tax liabilities, where the time frame may range from between four to seven years. This is due to the fact that HMRC can inspect tax records of a corporation and make an assessment as to any further tax that may be due, for anything up to six years after the end of the year of completion of the transaction. Any such time limits are entirely a matter of negotiation between the parties.

The seller may also place financial limits on the buyer by capping its total liability under the terms of the agreement at 50 per cent to 100 per cent of the total consideration received for the company or business, to ensure that it cannot be sued post completion for more than it received for the sale in the first place. Financial thresholds may also be placed on individual warranty claims to ensure that the seller is not required to action or defend any frivolous claims until all of the claims have reached a certain aggregate sum. These sums tend to be in the region of 0.5 per cent to 1 per cent of the total consideration received by the seller.

8.6.6.3 Entire agreement

An entire agreement clause is a common provision found in most English law commercial contracts. During the negotiating process, the selling party may make various representations to the potential buyer, most of which will be incorporated in the sale and purchase agreement. Consequently, the seller will not want to be liable for any representation that may have been made to the seller but for whatever reason was not incorporated into the agreement. As such, the seller will require some acknowledgement from the buyer that it has not relied on any other representation, and this is done via an entire agreement clause.

Note the following example of an entire agreement clause:

> *"Each party confirms that this Agreement sets out the entire agreement and understanding between the parties in relation to the transactions contemplated, and that it supersedes all previous agreements, arrangements and understandings between them or any of them with regard to such transactions and that that party is not entering into this Agreement or any of the arrangements contemplated in reliance upon any representation, undertaking or warranty, whether innocently or negligently made, of any person whether or not a party to this Agreement, other than as expressly set out in this Agreement. Nothing in this clause shall, however, operate to limit or exclude any liability for fraud."*

8.7 Effecting the transaction

It is a fairly straightforward procedure to transfer ownership in an acquisition of the shares in a company. The seller, regardless as to whether it is an individual or a company, will complete a stock transfer form, either in hard copy or an electronic version, which is handed over at the completion board meeting of the target, for its approval of the transfer. Other administrative issues will be dealt with at this meeting, such as the retirement of the old board of directors and the appointment of the new board. The relevant forms will be filed at Companies House, the purchaser of the shares will arrange for stamp duty to be paid, the stock transfer forms to be stamped and the internal register of members of the target company will be updated, and finally, new share certificates will be issued.

On an asset sale however, the process is not as simple. Once the buyer has identified the assets that it wishes to acquire, each of those assets must be individually transferred. For example:

(1) Land will be transferred by deed, transfer (form TR1), assignment or conveyance, depending on whether the land is freehold, leasehold, registered or unregistered.

(2) Machinery, vehicles and stock will be transferred by delivery.

(3) Goodwill, name and intellectual property rights by written assignment or registration.

(4) The employees will automatically transfer across due to **TUPE**. They will need to be notified of their new owner, be presented with the opportunity to object, and if any employment contracts are terminated, the relevant employees will, depending on their length of service have the opportunity to take action against either the buyer, the seller or both parties for unfair dismissal, unless the party responsible for the dismissal can show an economic, technical or organisational (ETO) reason for the dismissal and uses a fair process in dismissing the employee.

(5) Customer contracts are transferred.

8.7.1 Third party contracts

In a share sale, there are no changes to sales or supply contracts, because the contracting company remains the same, only the owners will change. Therefore, unless there is a change of control clause in a contract, these contracts will remain in place and will continue as normal. If there is a change of control provision within a key contract, then a negotiation will begin between the seller and the third party to ensure that a waiver is agreed so that the third party will not terminate the contract post completion.

In an asset sale any existing contract will have to be assigned or novated, as only the benefit of any contract can be assigned, not the burden. For example, if our scenario was an asset sale and not a share sale, and there was a supply contract in place for the supply of pastries between Choux on the table Ltd ("Choux"), and a third party, the burden of that contract is the supply of the pastries, and the benefit is the right that Choux has to be paid for the supply. As such, even if that contract is legally assigned to the new owner (see **s136 Law of Property Act 1925**) once the business of Choux is sold, the burden to supply those pastries will remain with Choux, even if essentially it has no means to make the pastries because all of its key assets have been sold on to Crepes. So, what are the options? For both the benefit and the burden of a contract to pass, the contract must be **novated**. This is carried out by a novation agreement, which is a short document which states that the new party – the buyer, in our case Crepes – has replaced Choux in this contract and that all of the burdens, benefits, obligations and liabilities have now been passed on to Crepes. All three parties will sign this novation agreement and normal contractual dealings will ensue between the third-party customer and Crepes.

Other alternative options are that Choux and the third-party customer terminate the agreement and the third party enters into a fresh agreement with Crepes, or the contract remains as it is, the benefit and the burden remain with Choux, who would receive payment for the supply of the pastries but would agree to hold that benefit on trust for Crepes. Crepes would then perform the burden of the contract, that is, bake and supply the pastries as agent for Choux. This may be a good temporary solution until a fresh contract can be negotiated.

8.8 Drafting a simple sale and purchase agreement

The structure of a sale and purchase agreement will be largely the same, for an asset sale or a share sale. Again, there are no hard rules as to how a contract should look but commercial contracts/sale and purchase agreements tend to follow the same format.

The document will have a front cover citing the names of the parties and the date upon which it comes into effect. The agreement will generally have a contents page, setting out the operative clauses and the schedules. The term "operative" simply refers to the main body of the agreement, which is everything up to the schedules. The agreement will start with the names and addresses of the parties:

"Parties

(1) FULL COMPANY NAME] incorporated and registered in England and Wales with company number [NUMBER] whose registered office is at [REGISTERED OFFICE ADDRESS] **(Seller)**

[or where there are several individual sellers:

The several persons whose names and addresses are set out in Schedule 1 **(Sellers)**]

(2) [FULL COMPANY NAME] incorporated and registered in England and Wales with company number [NUMBER] whose registered office is at [REGISTERED OFFICE ADDRESS] **(Buyer)**"

(Extract from Practical Law database)

The agreement may then contain what is referred to as the "Recitals". In this paragraph there will be some background to the deal, what is being bought and sold etc. You may then see some defined terms. Where a term or phrase is used repeatedly throughout the agreement, it will be given a shortened name with its meaning set out here. This is to make the agreement more reader-friendly and shorter in length. These definitions will be listed in alphabetical order, and they tend to start with a capital letter, which will be replicated throughout the agreement:

"1.1 The definitions and rules of interpretation in this clause apply in this agreement.

Accounts: the Group Accounts and the Individual Accounts.

Accounts Date: [DATE].

Business: the business carried on by the Company and the Subsidiaries [, namely [DESCRIPTION OF THE BUSINESS]], or any part of it.

Business Day: a day other than a Saturday, Sunday or public holiday in England when banks in London are open for business.

Buyer's Solicitors: [NAME OF BUYER'S SOLICITORS] of [ADDRESS OF BUY- ER'S SOLICITORS]."

(Extract from Practical Law database)

The rest of the agreement will set out exactly what is being sold and for how much. It will contain amongst other things, warranty and indemnity clauses. It will refer to each of the schedules of the agreement and deal with liabilities, confidentiality, entire agreement, where notices should be sent and have a jurisdiction clause. There will then be numerous schedules to the agreement dealing with the particulars of the sellers if applicable, tax, commercial terms, the warranties, the process for completion, details of properties, employees. The list is extensive and entirely deal-specific. It will conclude with an execution clause where all of the parties to the agreement will sign.

8.9 Tax implications

Let us go back to our scenario to look at the tax implications for the sellers – the Suchets and the buyer – Crepes.

8.9.1 Corporate seller

Patties Rock Ltd is a corporate seller. It has owned its 50 per cent shareholding in the target since its incorporation in 2004. Any chargeable gain that it makes as a result of the disposing of its 50 per cent shareholding in the target, will be capital in nature, which means that any such chargeable gain will be subject to corporation tax. However this disposal meets with the qualifying criteria for a tax exemption known as the substantial shareholding exemption. Therefore, it will pay no corporation tax on any chargeable gains that it makes on the sale of its shares in the target.

8.9.2 Individual seller

Leroy Suchet is an individual seller and any chargeable gains that he makes on the sale of his 50 per cent shareholding in the target will be subject to capital gains tax. Note that Leroy will qualify for **business asset disposal relief**. Leroy is disposing of his 50 per cent shareholding in his personal trading company, shares which he has held since incorporation. He is also a director of the target. As such, assuming he has not used his £1 million of gains lifetime cap, he will only pay capital gains tax at 10 per cent.

8.9.3 The buyer

Crepes is buying the shares in the target for cash consideration of £5 million. VAT is not applicable on share sales, but stamp duty is. Crepes will have to pay stamp duty at 0.5 per cent of the total consideration paid, which equals £25,000. However, the tax position of the target remains the same, the capital allowance regime is unaffected and trading losses can be carried forward and utilised throughout Crepes' group of companies.

8.10 Exchange and completion

Corporate acquisitions conclude in much the same way as a property transaction. The parties exchange contracts; in other words, two copies of the final sale and purchase agreement (with schedules and the disclosure letter and bundle) are signed – at this point there is a legally binding contract. The transaction is "complete" once the consideration and assets/shares have been transferred. On most occasions this will happen simultaneously, that is, on the same day. Occasionally, there is a gap between exchange of contracts and completion.

The entire process takes a great deal of organisation and cooperation between the buyer and the seller's lawyers. The process is managed via a completion agenda, which is prepared collaboratively beforehand, so that it is clear to both parties who is required to be present at the meeting, what documentation must be produced and where this event will happen. The lawyers on both sides will ensure that the correct authorities have been granted in order for the agreement to be executed, and if a certain individual is not there to sign in person, that the required power of attorney has been provided.

8.10.1 Corporate seller

As there is a corporate seller in our scenario, Patties Rock Ltd, it will have to hold a board meeting to approve the terms of the SPA, and the appropriate signatory will be appointed; this will undoubtedly be Mrs Suchet. Minutes will have to be taken of this board meeting and provided to Crepes' lawyers as evidence of her authority to act on behalf of the company. As this is a share sale, the target will also have to hold a board meeting to approve the transfer of its shares and registration of the new shareholders. The articles of both the corporate seller, and the target will be checked by the buyers to ensure all appropriate steps have been taken to approve the sale.

8.10.2 Corporate buyer

As Crepes is a corporate buyer and a plc, it must obtain the requisite approval from its shareholders and also hold a board meeting to approve the terms of the SPA and appoint a signatory. Certified minutes of this meeting will be handed over to the Suchets' lawyers. In a share sale and purchase, once the SPA and relevant documents have been signed and funds transferred, the only asset transferred between the parties are the shares themselves and that is carried out by a signed and duly stamped, stock transfer form and share certificates, but the new shareholders cannot exercise any rights until their names have been entered into the register of members, which is usually held by the target.

If the target does not hold its own register, then the new shareholders will have to wait until the shares are registered at Companies House before they can exercise any rights.

8.10.3 Completion of an asset sale and purchase

An asset sale will follow the same process, that is, the agenda will be prepared but far more documentation will have to be transferred in order to complete this transaction. To ensure the transfer of legal interests in the assets of a business to the buyer, the seller will need to produce at the completion meeting, amongst other documents, evidence of transfer of title such as conveyances, transfers, assignments of land and leases, assignments of goodwill, deeds and documents of title to the assets, financial records, duly executed releases of charges, and of course the signed SPA with disclosure letter and bundle. This is not a comprehensive list; it is entirely deal-specific. The buyer may also have to pay stamp duty land tax if any land is transferred in the transaction.

8.10.4 Conditional completion

Occasionally, sale and purchase agreements are signed and exchanged but completion is delayed until certain conditions have been fulfilled. This is often referred to as a conditional contract/agreement. The parties may require a conditional contract where various consents and/or approvals from regulatory authorities are required. In our scenario, as Crepes is a corporate buyer and a plc, it may require shareholders' consent to enter into the transaction, or clearance from the Competition and Markets Authority that the acquisition will not be subject to any lengthy investigations due to possible competition law issues. Equally, as the Suchets are selling the entire share capital of the target, as discussed earlier, the target may need to get the consent/waiver of any major suppliers or customers under the terms of any "change of control" provisions before Crepes is willing to complete the transaction.

8.10.5 Allocation of risk with conditional contracts

Once the conditional agreement has been signed, the buyer is contractually obliged to complete the purchase of the target company, regardless as to what events occur that might affect the target. As such, the agreement must be carefully drafted. Every clause should be conditional apart from the "conditionality" clause itself. It should clearly state what each party's obligation is in respect of each condition, the date by which the conditions should be met and each party's right to rescind and/ or sue for any breach of the conditions.

As the buyer will not have any control over the way in which the target is run during the conditional period, it will generally want the right to attend board meetings of the target and be kept informed of any day-to-day dealings of the target. Back to our deal, Crepes should insist on the following undertakings from the Suchets, ensuring that they:

- repeat any representations/warranties made, as at completion, just in case something occurs post exchange to make any of the warranties untrue; meaning the Suchets will be liable. (The Suchets may insist on having the right to update their disclosure letter to deal with any new issues arising in that period);
- carry on the business of the target as "normal" during the conditional period, for example, no major acquisitions, no major contracts being entered into or terminated, no hiring of firing of staff etc. unless Crepes gives prior consent;
- notify Crepes if there are any adverse material changes in the business, assets or profits of the target (referred to as a MAC clause); and
- agree to bear the risk of destruction or damage during the conditional period and hold insurance on trust for Crepes in this regard.

8.10.6 Post completion

Despite the fact that most of the work is over once the transaction has completed (and each party has celebrated the end of a long and no doubt arduous negotiation), the parties' lawyers will still have some final tasks to complete. Crepes' lawyers must ensure that the duly executed stock transfer forms are delivered to HMRC Stamp Office within 30 days, together with the transfer duty which is 0.5 per cent of the total consideration for the deal (rounded up to the nearest £5 – there is no charge if the shares are worth less than £1,000). As our deal is a share sale, Crepes' lawyers will also have to file the following documents, for both the target and Beautiful Bakes Ltd, at Companies House:

- a copy of any special resolutions;
- a copy of any new articles; and
- forms notifying the registrar or the new board of directors and secretary, the new registered office, and any change of accounting reference period.

Each party to the transaction will have its own full set of the documents used in the acquisition, sometimes referred to as a "Bible", and all Crepes now has to do is incorporate its new companies, Choux on the table Ltd and Beautiful Bakes Ltd within its group; whilst the Suchets can focus on building their other family business and enjoying the rewards earned from the sale of their company.

Knowledge checks!

(1) Which of the following are disadvantages of the franchise model from the point of view of the franchisee?

(a) An existing business model

(b) Use of intellectual property rights

(c) Lack of autonomy

(d) Goodwill to the franchisor

(2) What is the rate of stamp duty on the sale of shares?

(a) 0.5%

(b) 1%

(c) 5%

(d) 2%

8.11 Summary!

(1) Franchising is a structure by which a franchisor permits a franchisee to use the franchisor's business concept. The details vary substantially, but usually involve payment of a fee, licensing the franchisor's intellectual property to the franchisee, and often the supply of goods and/or service by the franchisor. The most important consideration for the franchisor is to maintain control over how the franchisee's business is run.

(2) A share sale is when the entire company is sold, with all of its assets and liabilities. The buyer will also acquire everything that the target company owns, including any subsidiary companies.

(3) An asset sale is when enough individual assets of a business are sold to a buyer to enable the business to continue to trade as a going concern post completion.

(4) Acquisitions can be financed by debt or equity.

(5) The most common preliminary documents used in acquisitions are heads of agreement/letters of intent, confidentiality agreements and due diligence questionnaires.

(6) Risk allocation begins with due diligence and continues throughout the trans- action with the negotiation of warranties and indemnities and vendor protection clauses.

(7) The parties must carefully consider the standard of disclosure that they accept, as this may affect any potential warranty claims post completion.

(8) The sale and purchase agreement will have a straightforward structure, with schedules setting out the commercials of the deal, including the warranties, the disclosure letter and bundle as well as the tax deed.

(9) There are many tax implications for both the buyer and the seller. The buyer will pay stamp duty/stamp duty land tax and possibly VAT, and the corporate seller may pay corporation tax. An individual seller will pay capital gains tax subject to any relevant exemptions and reliefs.

(10) Exchange occurs when the parties to the sale and purchase agreement sign and exchange the sale and purchase agreement. Completion will follow but it can be conditional where certain conditions must be met before assets and consideration are transferred.

Knowledge Checks – Answers

Chapter 1

(1) (a), (b) and (d)

Feedback:

The normal remedy in a civil law case is damages. Fines are used in **criminal** cases.

(2) (b) and (d)

Feedback:

The **Civil Procedure Rules** and the **Categories of Casino Regulations 2008** are examples of secondary legislation. Acts of Parliament are primary legislation.

Chapter 2

(1) (a)

Chapter 3

(1) (c)

(2) (a) and (d)

Feedback:

Acting for two clients who have a conflict of interest **is** permitted but there must be **informed** consent in writing; the parties must be competing for the same objective; and appropriate safeguards to protect confidential information must be in place. It must also be reasonable to act for both parties.

(3) (b)

Feedback:

The deposit payment is client money and must be paid into the client account.

(4) (a)

Chapter 4

(1)

Art 2	Right to life
Art 5	Right to liberty and security of person
Art 8	Right to respect for private and family life
Art 14	Prohibition of discrimination

(2) (a)

Chapter 5

(1) (b)

Feedback:

A local councillor is an internal client for the district council's in-house legal team. Jones Building (Wrexham) Ltd and Unison are both external clients.

(2)

CILEX Core Principle	SRA Principle
1	1
5	7
6	6

Chapter 6

(1) (c)

(2) (a)

Feedback:

The directors of the company, not the members, are responsible for its management.

Chapter 7

(1) (c)

Feedback:

Tor is a person of significant control because he actually exerts significant control through his wife Marian. Safia owns less than 25 per cent of the shares and Johann can only appoint one out of four directors which is not a majority. As a result, neither Safia or Johann are PSCs.

(2) (b)

Feedback:

Under **s51 CA 2006** a pre-incorporation contract made by a person will be treated as being made on behalf of the company if the promoter and the other party have expressly agreed beforehand that the contract is made with the company instead.

Chapter 8

(1) (c) and (d)

(2) (a)